A
SOUTHERLY
COURSE

Martha Hall Foose

A
SOUTHERLY
COURSE

Recipes & Stories from *Close to Home*

− MARTHA HALL FOOSE −

CLARKSON POTTER/PUBLISHERS
NEW YORK

FOR DONALD BENDER,

my husband and best friend, who gives our family our daily bread

Published in the United States by Clarkson Potter/Publishers,
an imprint of the Crown Publishing Group, a division of
Random House, Inc., New York.
www.clarksonpotter.com
www.crownpublishing.com

CLARKSON POTTER is a trademark and POTTER
with colophon is a registered trademark
of Random House, Inc.

Library of Congress Cataloging-in-Publication Data
Foose, Martha Hall.
   A southerly course / Martha Hall Foose. — 1st ed.
   Includes index.
   1. Cookery, American—Southern style. I. Title.
   TX715.2.S68F653 2010
   641.5975—dc22   2010022969
   ISBN 978-0-307-46428-6

Printed in China

Book design by Jennifer K. Beal Davis
Jacket photograph by Chris Granger

10 9 8 7 6 5 4 3 2 1

First Edition

*The South is a blend of the relentless and the abiding for me,
and an accumulation of ironies so acute and impenetrable that my
vagabond heart palpitates to make sense of them.*

—WILLIE MORRIS, *TERRAINS OF THE HEART*

*You've got to continue to grow, or you're just like
last night's cornbread—stale and dry.*

—LORETTA LYNN

Contents

Introduction

Mazy paths of rivers meander and by disposition I do the same.
My life, aside from little stints abroad and forays to the west and east coasts, has traveled a course close to the Mississippi River. I've lived up towards the narrow headwaters in Minnesota and down at its yawning mouth in New Orleans. As a child and now once more I live in its sprawling delta. Seemingly random events and choices conspired to bring me home again and keep me around.

This peculiarity, my trait of meandering, is markedly apparent in my cooking as well as in my conversation, a tendency to take switchbacks in time and place and even tastes. I have come to see that it is just my nature. Time and again I've wondered why it is I traverse these same roads over and over. Why do I reach for these same familiar ingredients? Why are my most cherished belongings made of cast iron? I think it is perhaps because we Southerners are homesick for the place in which we still live.

Sentimentality and a heaping spoonful of nostalgia flavor our dishes as much as black pepper and Worcestershire sauce do. It tastes good but sets us up for mockery. Our regional history, fraught by the economics of cotton and all that surrounds it, is difficult to maneuver and remain on solid footing. Communality through food in many ways has helped us as a region begin to reconcile ourselves with the past.

For the past two years I've spent my time touring through classic and modern kitchens, taking back-road rambles, and doing some in-depth explorations of venerated Southern ingredients. That has had me considering—and at times lamenting—how we feed ourselves, see ourselves, and portray ourselves. Peeking beneath the table's pall in the mythic South to see how its patent qualities of deep involvement with family, observance of ritual, and celebration of eccentricity play out around Southern food today has been quite a trip. It has taken me on an inner journey as well. My ambition to understand this mythologizing to which we Southerners are prone has had me up nights in the kitchen. The myths themselves seem to begin with stories told around tables.

And because so much of Southern living is spent in the kitchen, it is naturally the place to start. *A Southerly Course: Recipes & Stories from Close to Home* is a collection of recipes I gathered along my path. I hope it shares some of the flavors I believe will guide the way to a full-immersion baptism in the font of Southern culinary eccentricity, ingenuity, and creativity.

Passed, Plated & Shared

Rum Tum Tiddy—For Everyone

Fig Pecan Fondue—Warm All Over

Sweet Potato Wedges—Vinegar and Salt

Parish Olives—John Folse, Chef

Elsie's Welsh Rarebit—Miss Marple

Bacon Crackers—Corseted

Pickled Eggs and Sausages—Day on the Lake

Pickled Crawfish Tails—Bay Springs, Mississippi

Crawfish Bread—Turned Over

Oyster Patties—Pastry Cases

Oysters Casino—Along the Coast

Crispy Wontons—Joe's Treat

Escabèche—Spanish New Orleans

Crabmeat Casserolettes—Personal Taste

Burgundy Duck—Swamp Witches

Chicken Liver Spread—Bread and Butter Pickles

Rabbit Terrine—Dogwood Forks and Rufus Hussy

Doe Loin with Winter Biscuits—Highway 61

Venison Meatballs—Silver Fox Mustard

Soda Crackers—Toasty and Salty

RUM TUM TIDDY
For Everyone

Many a child home sick from school has been fed Rum Tum Tiddy—a soothing, warm concoction of tomato soup and melted cheese over toast. Where the dish got its funny name I don't know. I do know that it can hardly be said without a smile or guffaw. Here those comforting flavors are set up as a pick-up snack great for parties of all ages.

SERVES 4;
MAKES 16 PIECES

1 large egg, beaten

½ teaspoon Worcestershire
sauce

¼ pound Cheddar cheese,
grated (1 cup)

1 cup chopped pecan pieces

1 cup soft bread crumbs

1 tablespoon unsalted butter

2 tablespoons finely chopped
onion

1 cup (8-ounce can) tomato
sauce (I like Red Gold
brand)

1 cup grated Parmesan cheese

8 pickled okra pods, tops and
tips removed, sliced into
rounds

Heat the oven to 350°F. Butter an 8-inch square baking dish.

In a large bowl, combine the egg, Worcestershire sauce, Cheddar cheese, pecans, and bread crumbs.

In a medium skillet set over medium heat, melt the butter. Add the onion and cook until slightly browned, about 3 minutes. Add the tomato sauce and cook for 5 minutes. Pour the onion and tomato sauce over the bread-crumb mixture and stir together.

Spoon the tomato–bread-crumb mixture into the prepared baking dish and bake for 25 minutes or until firm. Cool for 10 minutes and cut into 16 squares.

Put the Parmesan cheese on a large plate. Coat all sides of the squares in the Parmesan. Place 1 round of pickled okra in the center of each square as a garnish.

To serve, skewer each square on a cocktail pick.

NOTES
• For a quick snack bite, cut white bread into cubes. Spread each cube with mayonnaise and sprinkle with grated Parmesan cheese or crumbled blue cheese. Bake in a 450°F. oven for 7 minutes or until the bread is toasty and the cheese is bubbly. Serve warm. You'll be surprised how fast these are gobbled up.

• Frank Ward O'Malley's contribution to the *Stag Cook Book* of 1922 is a riot of a recipe for Rum Tum Tiddy!

FIG PECAN FONDUE
Warm All Over

Rarely do I pull out any of the inexplicable number of fondue pots we got for wedding gifts. They just sit up on the ledge above my kitchen cabinets and collect dust. The fig preserves my girlfriend Jane Rule gifts to us also sit up on that shelf. I love her preserves. I love them so much that I always think I'm going to save them for a special occasion, and they end up collecting dust until the next jar arrives. It's ridiculous. This sweet, nutty cheese fondue uses both of these thoughtful gifts. On a chilly night, sharing this communal dish with friends makes you feel warm all over.

SERVES 6

½ cup dry white wine

½ cup fig preserves

¼ cup toasted pecans, ground

1 tablespoon fresh lemon juice

½ pound Gruyère cheese, grated (2 cups)

½ pound Emmentaler cheese, grated (2 cups)

2 tablespoons cornstarch

¼ teaspoon freshly ground black pepper

Grate of whole nutmeg

Cubes of pumpernickel bread, for dipping

Cubes of sourdough bread, for dipping

In a medium saucepan set over medium heat, combine the wine, fig preserves, pecans, and lemon juice. Cook, stirring often, until the preserves are melted.

In a medium bowl, combine the Gruyère, Emmentaler, cornstarch, pepper, and nutmeg. Stir the cheese mixture into the preserves one small handful at a time, making sure that each handful is completely melted before adding the next. The fondue can bubble a bit, but don't let it boil.

Transfer the cheese mixture to a warm fondue pot and keep warm over a burner. Stir occasionally. Serve right away with cubes of pumpernickel and sourdough bread for dipping.

SWEET POTATO WEDGES
Vinegar and Salt

Premium Number One Beauregards are a popular variety of sweet potato grown in Vardaman, Mississippi. There are ninety sweet-potato farms within forty miles of this town, which even boasts a Sweet Potato Street running right into Main Street. With twenty thousand acres under cultivation, sweet potatoes have to be the state's largest vegetable crop.

Here a tart-sweet treatment and a dusting of crystalline flakes of salt elevate the down-home goodness of my favorite Beauregards.

SERVES 6

⅓ cup balsamic vinegar

¼ cup (packed) dark brown sugar

3 tablespoons unsalted butter

2 teaspoons coarse flaky sea salt, plus extra for sprinkling

1 teaspoon red pepper flakes

6 medium sweet potatoes, peeled and cut lengthwise into 8 wedges

Heat the oven to 400°F.

In a large saucepan set over high heat, heat the vinegar, sugar, butter, salt, red pepper flakes, and 2 tablespoons water to boiling. Remove the pan from the heat, add the potato wedges, and toss to coat with the mixture.

Spread the potato wedges evenly on a foil-lined rimmed baking sheet. Roast, turning the wedges occasionally, for 45 minutes or until the potatoes are very tender and the glaze thickens. Remove from the oven and sprinkle the potatoes with additional salt, if desired. Let cool slightly before serving.

NOTES

• In 1987, Civil War buff and sweet-potato advocate Larry Rolston named this variety for Louisiana Confederate general P. G. T. Beauregard. Rolston's development of a high-yield and disease-resistant strain played a large role in revitalizing the sweet-potato industry.

• After harvest, sweet potatoes are allotted a curing time to allow any nicks to heal before shipping to market. Starch is also then converted to sugar, improving the flavor. The curing time can be as short as ten days in warm temperatures or as long as three weeks if it is cool.

PARISH OLIVES
John Folse, Chef

Born out on Cabanocey Plantation in rural St. James Parish in 1946, a young John Folse could probably never have imagined that the foods of his Louisiana upbringing would propel him around the world as a culinary ambassador. From humble beginnings and a belief in and commitment to the preservation of classic Cajun and Creole cuisines, Chef Folse has grown his culinary enterprises into a world-class operation. Since 2006, he has grown Arbequina olives on White Oak Plantation in Baton Rouge, Louisiana. Arbequina olives are the source of most California and Spanish olive oil. When the small, flavorful olives are ripe and cured, they are deep purple.

SERVES 8

1½ cups pitted brine-cured Arbequina or other black olives

1½ cups pitted brine-cured Alphonso or other green olives

¾ cup extra-virgin olive oil

¼ cup chopped fresh basil

¼ cup sherry vinegar

3 garlic cloves, thinly sliced

3 tablespoons chopped fresh parsley

½ teaspoon red pepper flakes

½ teaspoon ground cardamom

Grated zest and juice of 1 orange

Combine both kinds of olives, the olive oil, basil, vinegar, garlic, parsley, red pepper flakes, cardamom, and orange zest and juice in large heavy-duty resealable food-storage bag. Shake to blend the ingredients. Refrigerate for at least 1 day and up to 3 days, turning occasionally.

When ready to serve, transfer the olives and some of the marinade to a bowl and let stand for 1 hour to come up to room temperature.

NOTES

• Crisp baguette slices are a must served alongside for sopping up the spicy orange marinade.

• Chef Folse gives sage advice to young culinarians by sharing his philosophy: "Choose first the heritage of your people. Herein lies the spice and flavor of your very palate. Choose secondly the ingredients of your area. Herein lies the uniqueness of your creations." For a virtual tour of his olive orchard, visit http://www.jfolse.com/whiteoak/olive.htm

ELSIE'S WELSH RAREBIT
Miss Marple

Agatha Christie said of her grandmother, "Although a completely cheerful person, she always expected the worst of anyone and everything. And with almost frightening accuracy [she was] usually proved right." Her grandmother would say "I shouldn't be surprised if so-and-so was going on," Christie recalled. "And although with no grounds for these assertions, that was exactly what was going on." Sounds just like my grandmother Elsie.

Elsie fancied herself an adept armchair detective. She was thrilled when our neighbor was murdered. Wait—that might lend the wrong impression. She was saddened by the loss of life, certainly, but elated at the chance to do some sleuthing and speculating. She quickly deemed it a love triangle gone wrong, a day before the police figured it out. I can see her now, seated in her floral chintz wingback chair with feet propped on the hearth, reading a good mystery.

I must say that on early dark winter evenings I find myself right there in her favorite wingback, set about my guilty pleasure of working my way through The New Annotated Sherlock Holmes, *all 1,878 pages of it, with a plate of Elsie's rarebit to sustain me.*

SERVES 2

½ pound hard hoop cheese or extra-sharp Cheddar, grated (2 cups)

3 large eggs, separated

1 teaspoon whole-grain mustard

1 teaspoon Worcestershire sauce

½ teaspoon prepared horseradish

4 (½-inch-thick) slices *pain de campagne* or favorite rustic bread, lightly toasted

Heat the oven to 450°F.

In a large bowl, combine the cheese, egg yolks, mustard, Worcestershire sauce, and horseradish. Set aside.

Whip the egg whites until they hold stiff peaks. Add one third of the egg whites to the cheese mixture and stir to combine. Then fold in the remaining egg whites.

NOTES

- I like a big dollop of Major Grey's chutney on the side in winter or sliced tomatoes in summer.

- Hard hoop cheese is a waxed-rind cheese sometimes called rat trap cheese. Hoop cheese was widely available in groceries, cut to order on a special hoop cheese cutter. It is made by pressing fresh cheese curds into a round mold, hence the name "hoop."

Put the bread slices in a baking dish and spread the cheese mixture over them. Bake for 10 minutes or until the cheese is puffy and bubbly-brown around the edges.

BACON CRACKERS
Corseted

This may barely qualify as a recipe. It's not a time-saver, that's for sure, because these take forever to assemble. That doesn't stop my friend Neck-bone Red from dropping me a note to inquire if I am going to be bringing bacon crackers whenever she knows I'll be at a party. I have found in my hours devoted to crafting these irresistible bowtie-shaped snacks that the way to make a bunch of them at a time is to place them on a wire rack set over a rimmed baking sheet. The rack keeps the crackers from getting soggy while they bake and are corseted by the bacon.

SERVES 6

¾ pound thinly sliced bacon
(about 16 slices)
42 rectangular butter crackers
(such as Club or
Captain's or Waverly)

Heat the oven to 250°F.

Slice the bacon slices into thirds crosswise. Wrap each cracker with a piece of bacon, overlapping as little as possible. Place the wrapped crackers ½ inch apart on a wire rack set over a rimmed baking sheet or broiler pan. Bake for 1½ hours or until the bacon constricts the center of each cracker and becomes crisp. Remove the pan from the oven and allow the crackers to cool on the rack.

PICKLED EGGS AND SAUSAGES
Day on the Lake

In most bait shops throughout the South and beyond, big gallon jars of pink-tinted pickled eggs sit on counters next to smoked summer sausages. Here these two favorite fisherman's snacks are brined up together and make a perfect take-along lunch for a day out on the lake for the angler gourmand.

MAKES 1 PINT

24 quail eggs

About 2 cups white vinegar

16 cooked smoked beef cocktail sausages

1 (12.7-ounce) bottle champagne vinegar (1⅔ cups)

3 tablespoons finely chopped white onion

2 garlic cloves

½ teaspoon fresh dill

½ teaspoon yellow mustard seeds

3 teaspoons salt

¼ teaspoon cayenne pepper

NOTES

• Do not use aluminum or cast iron to boil eggs or make brine; the eggs will darken and take on a metallic taste if you do.

• When you first pour the white vinegar over the eggs, the spots on the shell will start to come off.

• A shortcut: Look for canned quail eggs packed in water at Asian markets. To use these, just pick up the recipe where the eggs are covered with the champagne vinegar mixture.

Check the eggs to make sure that none of them is cracked. Soak the eggs in warm water for 10 minutes, then inspect them well to make sure they are very clean. Put the eggs in a saucepan and cover with water by 1 inch. Bring the water to a boil, then remove the pan from the heat. Let the eggs sit for 10 minutes, giving them a gentle stir every now and then. Pour off the water, cover the eggs with white vinegar (about 2 cups), and refrigerate for 12 hours.

Pour off the vinegar and dissolved eggshell. Rinse the eggs well in cold water. Peel the eggs under running water, removing any remaining shell and membrane, and then you are ready to pickle them.

In a medium skillet over medium heat, cook the sausages for 3 minutes or until slightly plumped and beginning to brown. Put the sausages and eggs in a pint jar.

In a small saucepan set over medium heat, bring the champagne vinegar, onion, garlic, dill, mustard seeds, salt, and cayenne pepper to a simmer. Pour the hot brine over the eggs and sausages to cover. Cool to room temperature, cover, and refrigerate for 2 days or up to a week.

PICKLED CRAWFISH TAILS
Bay Springs, Mississippi

The Jasper County village of Bay Springs, twenty miles from Laurel, Mississippi, was named in 1901 for an artesian spring flowing from the trunk of a bay laurel; it flows still to this day. I always think of that town when I make this dish.

Introducing freshwater crawfish to leaves from a bay laurel, traditional pickling spices, and tarragon vinegar prepares them to sit on top of salads and toasts.

SERVES 6

2 (12-ounce) packages frozen cleaned and peeled crawfish tails, defrosted

1 small onion, halved and thinly sliced

½ cup tarragon vinegar

¼ cup olive oil

3 garlic cloves, thinly sliced

6 whole black peppercorns

2 whole allspice berries

½ teaspoon coriander seeds

½ teaspoon celery seeds

½ teaspoon fennel seeds

½ teaspoon mustard seeds

½ teaspoon dill seeds

¼ teaspoon red pepper flakes

4 bay leaves

1 cinnamon stick

4 whole cloves

1 star anise

1 tablespoon sugar

½ teaspoon minced peeled fresh ginger

Put the crawfish tails and onion in a large glass container.

Bring 1 cup water, the vinegar, olive oil, garlic, peppercorns, allspice, coriander seeds, celery seeds, fennel seeds, mustard seeds, dill seeds, red pepper flakes, bay leaves, cinnamon stick, cloves, star anise, sugar, and ginger to a boil in a nonreactive saucepan. Cook for 5 minutes. Pour the hot liquid over the crawfish and onion. Let cool, then cover, and refrigerate for 24 hours.

NOTES

• If you like, 1½ pounds peeled boiled shrimp can be substituted for the crawfish in this recipe.

• I like to serve these with assorted pickled peppers and vegetables for a spicy snack with cocktails or on top of leafy green salads. Quite good stirred into pasta salads, too.

• This pickling-spice mixture works well with many recipes that call for pickling spice. Make a big old batch of this spice blend (minus the fresh ginger) to give as gifts for friends who are into home canning.

CRAWFISH BREAD
Turned Over

Most crawfish bread recipes are made with a hollowed-out loaf of French bread. Here the crawfish filling is enrobed in a tender ricotta dough, making these more like turnovers. Whether you make them small for pick-up party food or a more substantial calzone-like size, these are perfect for tailgating or game-day parties.

MAKES 8 TURNOVERS

DOUGH

1 cup ricotta cheese

2 large eggs

¼ cup whole milk

½ teaspoon garlic salt

3 cups unbleached all-purpose flour

4 teaspoons baking powder

FILLING

1 pound peeled crawfish tails, chopped

¾ cup diced onion

¼ pound smoked Gouda cheese, shredded (1 cup)

½ cup grated carrot (about 1 medium)

½ cup chili sauce (I use Heinz)

¼ cup diced green bell pepper

1 teaspoon Worcestershire sauce

1 large egg, beaten

MAKE THE DOUGH. In a small bowl, mix together the ricotta, eggs, milk, and garlic salt.

In a separate medium bowl, combine the flour and baking powder. Using a fork, stir the ricotta mixture into the flour mixture to form a shaggy dough. Gather the dough together with your hands and press it into a flat disk about 8 inches in diameter. Wrap in plastic wrap and refrigerate while making the filling.

MAKE THE FILLING. In a large bowl, combine the crawfish tails, onion, cheese, carrot, chili sauce, bell pepper, and Worcestershire sauce.

Heat the oven to 400°F. Line 2 baking sheets with parchment paper or spray with nonstick cooking spray.

Using a sharp knife, cut the dough disk into 8 wedges. Gather each wedge and shape it into a ball. Roll each ball into a 7- to 8-inch round. Place ½ cup of the filling in the center of each round. Fold the dough over the filling to form half-moon shapes. Using the tines of a fork, press the edges to seal. Place the turnovers on the prepared baking

sheets. Brush the top of each turnover with beaten egg. With a sharp knife, cut a small slit in the top of each turnover to let the steam escape while baking.

Bake the turnovers for 30 to 35 minutes, rotating the baking sheets from upper to lower halfway through baking to ensure even cooking. Remove the baking sheets from the oven and transfer the turnovers to a wire rack to cool for 5 minutes before serving.

OYSTER PATTIES
Pastry Cases

Oyster patties are much more sophisticated than their name and are to me one of the most elegant dishes to serve for a seated dinner, not that we have those often. They also make a wonderful offering for a more casual soiree, served from a chafing dish surrounded by the little pastry cases ready to be filled with the warm creamed oysters.

SERVES 6

PASTRY CASES
3½ cups unbleached bread flour

1 cup cake flour (not self-rising)

1 tablespoon sugar

1 teaspoon salt

1 cup (2 sticks) unsalted butter, cut into 16 pieces, cold

1 teaspoon cider vinegar

NOTES
• If you are a hostess pressed for time, pick up frozen puff pastry shells at the grocer.

• The vinegar helps make the pastry more tender.

• The pastry cases can be made 1 day in advance or frozen unbaked for 1 month.

• If you like, cut 3-inch rounds of dough and top each round with a circle with the center cut out (like a doughnut) and bake to form more elegant patty shells (or you can just buy some frozen ones).

MAKE THE PASTRY CASES. In a large bowl, stir together the bread flour, cake flour, sugar, and salt. Toss the chunks of butter into the flour and make sure each piece is coated with it. Combine the vinegar with 1 cup cold water and stir into the flour mixture while lightly tossing the ingredients to moisten them evenly. Gather the dough into a ball.

On a lightly floured surface, pat and roll the dough into a neat rectangle that's about ½ inch thick. Fold the dough into thirds like a business letter, wrap in plastic wrap, and refrigerate for at least 30 minutes.

Unwrap the dough and place it on a floured work surface with the folded side towards you. Roll the folded dough into a rectangle and again fold the dough into thirds. Repeat this process two times. The dough will be slightly marbled-looking with streaks of butter running through it. Wrap the dough in plastic and let it chill for 1 hour.

OYSTER FILLING

6 tablespoons (¾ stick) unsalted butter

6 tablespoons unbleached all-purpose flour

⅓ cup finely chopped shallots

⅓ cup finely chopped celery

1 tablespoon finely chopped garlic

1 pint shucked oysters, coarsely chopped, liquor reserved

1 cup clam juice

1 bay leaf

Sprig of fresh thyme

1½ teaspoons salt

¼ teaspoon cayenne pepper

3 tablespoons heavy cream

1 tablespoon dry sherry

2 tablespoons chopped fresh parsley

Unwrap the dough and place it on a floured work surface. Roll it out to a ¼-inch thickness and cut it into 4-inch squares with a sharp knife. Place the squares 3 inches apart on a baking sheet and chill for 1 hour.

Heat the oven to 400°F.

Bake the pastries for 10 minutes or until puffed and golden. Remove the pastries to a cooling rack.

MAKE THE OYSTER FILLING. In a medium skillet set over medium heat, melt the butter. Sprinkle the flour over the butter and whisk to combine. Cook, stirring constantly, for 3 minutes or until the roux is lightly golden. Add the shallots, celery, and garlic and cook until softened, about 4 minutes. Add the oyster liquor and the clam juice to the roux, along with the bay leaf, thyme, salt, and cayenne pepper, and cook, stirring, until the mixture thickens, about 4 minutes. Add the heavy cream, sherry, and parsley and cook for 3 minutes or until very thick. Add the oysters and cook, stirring, just until the edges begin to curl, 3 to 4 minutes. Discard the bay leaf.

To serve, make an indentation in the center of each pastry square using the back of a spoon. Spoon the oyster filling into the center of each pastry. Serve at once.

OYSTERS CASINO
Along the Coast

Eleven casinos dot the Mississippi beachfront from Biloxi to Bay St. Louis. I'm not too much on gambling—I'm poor and my luck isn't so great—but I have a friend, Dale, who works for a large casino concern and he invited me there recently for a big music event. With some time to kill I decided to try my luck in the casino. Cards are not my thing and I like gawking at people, so roulette seemed the best game for me. When the croupier, Twayla, set the ball to spinning it hopped off the wheel, missing the thirty-eight pockets, and went right down the front of my blouse. The guy next to me asked me my bra size and it came up on the next spin. People think I make this kind of thing up but Dale saw the casino security tape to prove it!

Seventeen natural oyster reefs are managed by the Mississippi Department of Marine Resources along the Mississippi Sound, which runs ninety miles east to west from Waveland to the Dauphin Island Bridge. On the south side, the Gulf Islands National Seashore separates the sound from the true Gulf of Mexico. As I write this the fate of the Mississippi Gulf Coast, its oysters, and its tourism industry is under siege from that catastrophic oil spill. I am betting on the resilience of these folks; they have come back from the brink of disaster before.

SERVES 4

24 shucked oysters, on the half shell
4 thick slices smoky bacon
2 tablespoons unsalted butter
¼ cup finely chopped red bell pepper
¼ cup finely chopped green bell pepper
¼ cup finely chopped shallots
¼ cup finely chopped celery
Salt and freshly ground black pepper

Heat a grill to medium-low or heat the oven to 500°F.

Arrange the oysters on a large rimmed baking sheet and keep cold in the refrigerator.

In a medium skillet set over medium heat, cook the bacon until crisp, about 5 minutes. Transfer to paper towels to drain and cut crosswise into 1-inch pieces. Reserve the bacon drippings in the pan.

1 tablespoon chopped fresh
parsley
2 teaspoons chopped fresh
oregano
Lemon wedges, for serving

Melt the butter in the skillet with the drippings over medium-high heat. Add the bell peppers, shallots, and celery; cook, stirring often, until softened, about 5 minutes. Season with salt and pepper, and stir in the parsley and oregano. Spoon the mixture over the oysters, and top with the bacon.

Using tongs, transfer the oysters to the grate and grill over a moderately low fire for 7 to 10 minutes, or until just cooked through. Alternatively, roast the oysters on the baking sheet for 7 to 10 minutes. Transfer to a platter and serve at once with lemon wedges.

CRISPY WONTONS
Joe's Treat

As is the case in many small towns, the most exotic fare found in my county is the Chinese-American buffet. My son, Joe, just loves the one at China Blossom in Greenwood. The family farm, Pluto, is forty-eight miles from town, so it's quite a commitment to make the round trip. Every so often for movie night, I make a pile of these crisp-fried, creamy, seafood-filled pouches for him and his pal Lola and we just stay out at Pluto.

MAKES 30; SERVES 6

1 (8-ounce) package cream cheese, softened
6 ounces chopped shelled cooked shrimp or crabmeat, or 1 (6-ounce) can, rinsed and drained
2 green onions, white and green parts, finely chopped
2 tablespoons unbleached all-purpose flour
1 teaspoon soy sauce
30 square wonton wrappers
1 large egg beaten with 1 teaspoon water
Vegetable oil, for frying
Sweet and Sour Sauce (recipe follows)

In a small bowl, combine the cream cheese, seafood, green onions, flour, and soy sauce. Chill for 30 minutes.

Put 1 teaspoon of the seafood filling in the center of each wonton wrapper. Use a pastry brush or your finger to paint a line of egg wash around the edge of each wrapper. Gently fold the wrapper over the filling to form a triangle, lightly press out any air, and press the edges to seal them.

In a large pot or deep-fryer, heat at least 2 inches of oil to 325°F. Fry the wontons in small batches, turning as needed to brown evenly, for 2 minutes or until crisp. Transfer them to a rack set over a paper-towel-lined baking sheet to drain. (If desired, keep warm on the cooling rack in a 200°F. oven.) Serve with sweet and sour sauce for dipping.

SWEET AND SOUR SAUCE

MAKES ABOUT ¾ CUP

½ cup apricot preserves

¼ cup rice vinegar

1 tablespoon soy sauce

2 tablespoons hot chili sauce
    (optional)

Combine the preserves, vinegar, soy sauce, and hot chili sauce (if desired) in a bowl.

ESCABÈCHE
Spanish New Orleans

Alejandro O'Reilly was the Irish-born Spanish general sent to bring the Louisiana Territories to order after France ceded the region to Spain. Throughout New Orleans cooking you will see an easy blending of French and Spanish culinary styles, easier perhaps than the actual history of the Louisiana Territory.

This escabèche is inspired by the history of that city I love to visit. From the Irish Channel to the funky music district of Frenchmen Street, the Spanish influence can still be tasted.

SERVES 6

½ cup unbleached all-purpose flour
3 pounds catfish fillets
About 1 cup olive oil
2 large yellow onions, thinly sliced
2 carrots, thinly sliced
4 garlic cloves, thinly sliced
2 hot peppers, seeded and thinly sliced
2 bay leaves
Sprig of fresh thyme
12 whole black peppercorns
½ teaspoon salt
¼ teaspoon red pepper flakes
Pinch of saffron threads
½ cup sherry vinegar

NOTES
- Stack this marinated fish on toast for delicious tapas.
- In 1769 Governor O'Reilly had six French loyalists executed at the foot of what is now the groovy music club strip, Frenchmen Street.

Put the flour in a large shallow dish; dredge the fish in the flour to coat lightly.

In a large skillet or sauté pan, heat about ¼ cup of the oil over medium-high heat. Add the fish in batches and cook until brown on both sides and just cooked through, about 10 minutes, adding more oil as needed for each batch. Transfer the fish to paper towels to drain.

Wipe the skillet clean and heat ¼ cup of the oil over medium heat. Add the onions, carrots, garlic, peppers, bay leaves, thyme, peppercorns, salt, red pepper flakes, and saffron. Cook, stirring occasionally, until the vegetables are soft and brown, 8 to 10 minutes. Remove from the heat and stir in the vinegar. Let cool completely.

Put the fish in a glass baking dish. Pour the cooled vegetable mixture over the fish, cover tightly, and refrigerate for at least 12 and up to 24 hours.

CRABMEAT CASSEROLETTES
Personal Taste

I really enjoy the flavor of sweet potato and fennel. If you're not a fan of the latter's licorice-like taste, substitute caraway seeds. I love the way seafood's sweetness is enhanced by them. These individual casseroles bring the flavors of Mississippi's hills and Gulf Coast together quite nicely.

SERVES 6

4 cups (½-inch) diced sweet potato

8 tablespoons (1 stick) unsalted butter

1 cup half-and-half, or more if needed

2 garlic cloves, minced

½ pound Monterey Jack cheese, grated (2 cups)

¼ cup chopped fresh parsley

¼ cup chopped green onions, white and green parts

½ teaspoon fennel seeds

½ teaspoon cayenne pepper

½ pound fresh crabmeat

Paprika

NOTE

• For those who really dig that licorice flavor, add ¼ teaspoon aniseed.

• Sprinkle in 1 tablespoon chopped fennel fronds if you have fennel around.

Heat the oven to 400°F.

In a large pot of boiling water, cook the sweet potatoes until soft, about 8 minutes. Drain well and return to the pot. Add the butter and let it melt over the hot potatoes. Add the half-and-half and mash it with the potatoes, mixing until they are smooth and not stiff and adding more half-and-half if needed. Add the garlic, cheese, parsley, green onions, fennel seeds, and cayenne. Fold in the crabmeat.

Put the mixture into greased individual ramekins or a single baking dish and sprinkle the top with paprika. Bake for 20 minutes or until heated through and beginning to brown.

BURGUNDY DUCK
Swamp Witches

A brace of ducks dangled from a nail hammered into the porch beam as Lila regaled me, on an icy night right after New Year's, with tales of the Swamp Witches, six accomplished women dedicated to hunting and to each other. For more than a decade, these ladies have gathered a couple of times each year out at Ward Lake Hunting Club, a 6,500-acre preserve running right along the Mississippi River. They eschew newfangled duck boats, favoring canoes to haul their decoys and gear. Eyeing the sky from beneath the brims of their chic tartan-banded hats, these experienced hunters can call a mallard by its wing action. They aren't pantywaists.

Lila is what you might call a spitfire, an avid fox hunter and competitive show jumper all of about five feet tall, with a fiery mane, emerald eyes, and a wicked sense of humor. She has trained her seven-year-old retriever, Tuff, to do many things, from stopping dead in his tracks at her command to tossing a biscuit posed upon his nose into the air before gobbling it up.

One dinner, in the course of telling a tale about a previous season's hunt, Lila slapped the table for emphasis and said "kennel-up" as part of the story. With that, Tuff instantly bounded up on the table, sending wineglasses flying. We all about fell out of our chairs with laughter as Tuff stood baffled on the dinner table in a puddle of Burgundy.

This recipe is dedicated to the Swamp Witches: Allison, Susan, Kate, Lind, Leigh, and Lila; I have fallen under their spell.

SERVES 4

2 (1-pound) wild ducks, dressed, or 8 (4-ounce) duck breasts

Salt

4 tablespoons (½ stick) unsalted butter

¼ cup unbleached all-purpose flour

2 cups chicken broth

1 cup red wine, preferably Burgundy

2 shallots, chopped

2 bay leaves

2 cups chopped white mushrooms

Freshly ground black pepper

Melba toast, for serving

NOTE
• To learn more about the Swamp Witches, visit www.swampwitches.com.

Put the ducks in a large pot, cover them with water, and season the water with salt. Simmer over medium heat for 30 minutes. Drain, remove the ducks, and pat them dry.

Return the pot to the stove, add the butter, and melt over medium-high heat. Add the ducks and cook, turning occasionally, for 15 minutes or until brown on all sides. Transfer them to a plate and set aside to cool. Remove the skin, discard the bones, and shred the meat.

Add the flour to the pot and cook, stirring, for 2 minutes. Stir in the broth, wine, shallots, and bay leaves. Add the mushrooms and season with salt and pepper. Cook, stirring, for 5 minutes or until the mixture is slightly thick and beginning to bubble. Return the duck meat to the pot and cover. Reduce the heat to low and cook for 1 hour. Discard the bay leaves.

Serve warm heaped on Melba toast.

CHICKEN LIVER SPREAD
Bread and Butter Pickles

What does this look like, chopped liver? Actually it looks like a mosaic. Like great Southern folk art, this recipe takes something humble and puts it on a pedestal so it can be admired. Chicken livers are so inexpensive and can be transformed into a luxury with the addition of a poultry seasoning blend, onions, butter, and bacon. Lining the bowl with plastic wrap and taking some artistic license with bread and butter pickles and pimientos means that this spread, when inverted for serving, becomes something to behold.

MAKES 2 CUPS

1 pound chicken livers, well trimmed and thoroughly rinsed

½ cup chopped onion

½ teaspoon poultry seasoning

8 tablespoons (1 stick) unsalted butter, softened

6 slices bacon, cooked and crumbled

1 teaspoon dry mustard

¼ teaspoon salt

¼ teaspoon freshly ground black pepper

¼ cup cold chicken broth, preferably homemade

Bread and butter pickles, for garnish

Diced pimientos, for garnish

Baguette slices, for serving

In a medium saucepan, combine 1½ cups water with the chicken livers, onion, and poultry seasoning. Simmer for 10 minutes. Remove the pan from the heat and allow the livers to cool in the liquid. When the livers are cool, drain well.

Put the livers, butter, bacon, mustard, salt, and pepper in the bowl of a food processor. Pulse until the mixture is smooth, adding the chicken broth as needed to make a smooth thick paste.

Line a 2-cup bowl with plastic wrap and spray with nonstick cooking spray. Arrange the pickle slices and pimientos in a mosaic or other decorative pattern in the bowl. Spoon the liver mixture over the pickles. Press lightly and tap several times on the counter to knock out any air bubbles. Cover and refrigerate for at least 2 hours.

To unmold, dip the bowl in hot water for a minute and invert onto the serving platter; discard the plastic wrap. Serve with the baguette slices.

NOTES

• Lucky for me I'm married to an artisan baker. Not only does he smell like a warm, freshly baked loaf of bread much of the time, but he also makes me baguettes. When I ask nicely, he will make them with wild rice cooked in chicken broth to serve alongside this beautiful spread.

• Bread and butter pickles let the rich iron flavor of the livers come through, whereas small dills can cover up their flavor.

RABBIT TERRINE
Dogwood Forks and Rufus Hussy

Rufus Hussy was perhaps the greatest slingshot shooter who ever lived. Known far and wide as the Beanshooter Man, Mr. Hussy was brought up using his slingshot skills to put dinner on the table for his eleven brothers and sisters. He could spot the perfect fork in a dogwood tree for making a beanshooter and numbered the ones he made; the last one was number 15,864.

As Rufus could attest, rabbits are easy game for a practiced shooter. This year my father made a beanshooter for my son, Joe, out of a forked piece of dogwood and a tourniquet from the hospital where he works. It was wrapped up under the Christmas tree with a one-pound bag of dried beans. If Joe practices enough with those beans, he might bag a rabbit with a marble by next Christmas. I know what I'll make.

SERVES 4

1 cup unbleached all-purpose flour

Salt and freshly ground black pepper

2 young rabbits, dressed and cut into 6 to 8 pieces, rib cages discarded

¼ cup olive oil

1 onion, thinly sliced

1 celery stalk, finely chopped

1 small carrot, finely chopped

2 tablespoons capers, rinsed

3 tablespoons golden raisins

¼ cup honey

½ cup cup wine vinegar

1 cup chicken broth

Heat the oven to 325°F.

Put the flour on a plate and season with salt and pepper. Stir to combine. Season the rabbit with salt and pepper, then lightly coat it with the seasoned flour.

Heat the oil in a large ovenproof or cast-iron skillet set over medium-high heat. Add the rabbit in batches and brown it on all sides, about 15 minutes per batch. Transfer the rabbit to a plate and set aside.

Reduce the heat under the skillet to medium. Add the onion, celery, and carrot and cook for about 5 minutes. Add the capers and raisins and cook, stirring, for about 5 minutes. Add the rabbit back to the pan.

RECIPE CONTINUES

NOTES

- I serve this straight out of the loaf pan with sourdough bread.

- A rabbit's foot carried in the pocket was a lucky charm in the early twentieth century; examples mounted in silver made in America but sold in England were advertised as "the left hind foot of a rabbit killed in a country churchyard at midnight, during the dark of the moon, on Friday the 13th of the month, by a cross-eyed, left-handed, red-headed bow-legged Negro riding a white horse—this we do not guarantee." *Folk-Lore* 19 (1908) 296.

- One hundred marbles for a dollar is a pretty cheap price for ammo—or good luck.

In a small bowl, combine the honey and vinegar. When the honey has dissolved, pour the mixture over the rabbit. Add the broth and season with salt and pepper.

Cover and bake for 1½ hours or until the meat is very tender and falling off the bone. Remove the rabbit from the pan, and when cool enough to handle, diligently remove the bones. Transfer the meat and all the vegetables in the skillet to a large loaf pan. Cool and chill overnight.

DOE LOIN WITH WINTER BISCUITS
Highway 61

"Up until the time I was eleven or twelve years old, people would ask me where I was from and I'd always say Leland. I never wanted to claim Texas . . . I loved Mississippi. All the blues in the world came from there."

A tall, lanky albino almost certainly isn't what springs to mind when you think of a blues guitar-man. But, once you listen to Johnny Winter, all that changes. His parents lived in Leland, Mississippi, before moving to Beaumont, Texas. As a kid Johnny spent his summers in the small Mississippi town on Highway 61—the Blues Highway.

These biscuits bake up a little on the pale side, but that's all right.

SERVES 6

VENISON

2 venison tenderloins (about ¾ pound each)

½ cup molasses

¼ cup cider vinegar

¼ cup apple juice

¼ cup honey mustard (or 2 tablespoons honey and 2 tablespoons Dijon mustard)

2 garlic cloves

½ teaspoon ground ginger

¼ teaspoon freshly grated nutmeg

½ teaspoon chopped fresh rosemary

2 teaspoons vegetable oil

PREPARE THE VENISON. In a large bowl or 1-gallon resealable food-storage bag, combine the venison, molasses, vinegar, apple juice, honey mustard, garlic, ginger, nutmeg, and rosemary. Stir or turn the meat to disperse the spices. Refrigerate for at least 4 hours or overnight.

Remove the venison from the marinade and pat dry; reserve the marinade. Heat a medium cast-iron skillet over medium heat until hot. Pour the oil into the skillet and add the tenderloins. Sear the tenderloins, turning to cook all sides, until evenly browned, about 8 minutes. Remove the tenderloins from the pan. Pour the reserved marinade into the skillet and cook, stirring constantly, until the mixture boils for 1 minute. Return the tenderloins to the skillet, turning to coat them in the sauce.

RECIPE CONTINUES

BISCUITS

2 cups unbleached all-
    purpose flour

3 teaspoons baking powder

½ teaspoon baking soda

½ teaspoon salt

1 cup sour cream

MAKE THE BISCUITS. Heat the oven to 450°F.

Mix together the flour, baking powder, baking soda, and salt. Add the sour cream and mix until a soft dough forms. With well-floured hands, shape the dough into 12 balls. Put them on a baking sheet and flatten slightly. Bake for 9 to 12 minutes, until barely browned.

Transfer the tenderloins to a serving platter and pour the sauce over the meat. Allow the meat to rest for 10 minutes before slicing it thin. Surround the meat with the warm biscuits and serve.

NOTE
• You can watch Johnny play the blues on YouTube while your biscuits bake. I especially like the clip where he performs with legendary blues man Muddy Waters.

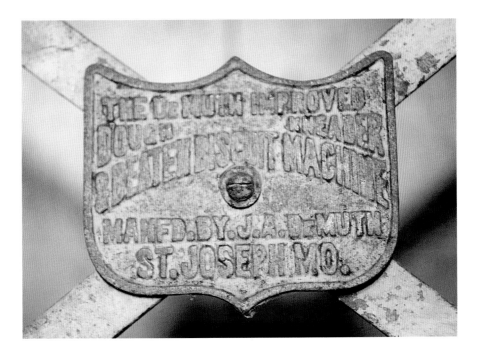

Yes, Deer: WHITETAILS

In 1929, two years after the great flood, there were thought to exist nowhere in Mississippi, except in very limited areas of the Delta, numbers of deer large enough to justify hunting. The ideas of Aldo Leopold, the father of wildlife management, were carried out by the state, which purchased deer to release across its forested acres. By the early 1940s the deer population had grown to more than an estimated 10,000, with more than a third of those thought to be roaming the rivered counties of Issaquena, Sharkey, Warren, and Yazoo. The first antlerless deer season in Mississippi was held in 1961.

Today *Odocoileus virginianus* has a population across the United States that is thought to exceed 30 million, with an estimated herd of 1.75 to 2 million ranging across Mississippi. The Magnolia State has the highest density of whitetails in the country, equaling out to be about one deer plus a hind-quarter or backstrap for every man, woman, and child. Only Texas is thought to have a greater number of deer—and Texas is five times the size of Mississippi.

I had tried to steer clear of anything that had to do with deer hunting for many years. I guess I had some issues about it. Not ethical. I'm fine with hunting. I grew up around it and understand that without good management practices, overpopulation can lead to disease and starvation for the herd. I also like to eat venison. No, this was a personal aversion.

When I was in seventh grade I started to go to school in Jackson, about sixty miles away. I had thought long and hard about the best outfit to wear on the first day of school in a big-city school. After a sleepless night I got up, got dressed, performed some maneuvers with a curling iron, and hopped in the car with my mother. The car would not start. "OK, I won't look too bumpkin going to school in my dad's truck. I mean, nobody knows me and I will just sort of slip in," I thought. My mom took the wheel and we headed for Jackson.

Around Bentonia I was bored and opened the glove box. Out fell a little bottle of a substance called Tink's Doe-in-Rut Buck Lure. Formulated from doe emissions—really—it is used to mask a hunter's scent and attract randy bucks. It is not in any way what a seventh-grade girl on her first day of school in town wants to smell like. In fact, it is something that can turn a thirteen-year-old girl into a sobbing, heaving wreck when spilled on a new, red-trimmed Tanner blouse and matching madras walking shorts. My mother floored it to the first truck stop she could find. I washed and washed with soap from the wall-mounted dispenser in the restroom. Dripping, I looked around for some paper towels. Nothing. On the wall was one of those hot air hand-dryers. Let's just say that once that hot air hit the now widely dispersed Tink's, it lit the place up.

Inconsolable is what I was. We sped to McRae's department store. Of course, they weren't open yet, this being seven thirty in the morning. My momma tapped on the windows with her car key until someone came to the door. God knows what they thought seeing this bawling girl in the passenger seat with a near-bout hysterical woman at the door. Within minutes, with a promise not to touch anything, I was in the store looking in the Junior Missy collection. I picked out something not nearly as perfect as my original ensemble. I made it to school and through the day not knowing if my scent had died down or if I had just become immune to it by then. I did seem quite popular with the boys, though.

My father has always been an avid hunter. He has guided many young men on their first hunts. My father's journals, which he writes each season, are epic romances between man and nature. There is simply nowhere in the world he would rather be than in the same woods he rambled as a child.

The ritualistic behavior begins with the arrival of "the Rut," a special issue of *Field & Stream,* a favored sporting magazine. Scouting trips for tracks and twilight levee rides consume early autumn. But the workup begins in earnest when that magazine arrives late in the fall. Vacation days from work are claimed and sick days added to the tally once dates for the season are announced by the Game and Fish Commission.

I eventually married a man whom my father taught to hunt, and the sport is now a passion for Donald, too. I've never taken to hunting, but I have embraced and share in the seasonal rituals. I keep my sharing mostly to the kitchen. When that magazine issue arrives, the race to get the deep-freeze cleared out and all of last year's deer meat used up before the next season's arrival is in full swing. Right after deer season my excitement for the new season's harvest is at its height. Then I think I want to save some for the grill in the summer, some for smoked sausage for gumbo when it gets cold . . . then there it is, deer season again.

A 175-pound deer carcass is a lot to confront. After it's been field dressed, the deer is hung by the back legs from pulleys at the tractor shed. It is then skinned with the tenderloins and backstrap (loins) removed. Many people then contend with the rest of it themselves. I turn to professionals.

About seven miles outside Yazoo City, south of town, Teresa and Charlie Milner have a thriving seasonal business, now in its seventeenth year, processing deer meat October through January. Their big metal building on hilly, curvy Fletcher's Chapel Road was a timely expansion. Charlie learned how to butcher back in 1971 when he was working part-time at the Sunflower grocery store. He always butchered his own deer. Soon friends started to show up wanting him to work on theirs. He took it up as a sideline. The first year he dismantled twenty-five deer in Teresa's kitchen at home. She put her foot down. The operation moved to a spare shed, and about four years ago they opened up this new place about 150 yards down the road.

Teresa is a beautiful woman with eyes like Lynda Carter from the *Wonder Woman* TV show. At first I thought Donald and my dad took their deer there because they had a little crush on her. And they do, but the real reason is because the Milners do such a good job. She checks in the meat brought in all day by hunters who like to look in those blue eyes and tell her all about it—how it was right at dawn, how I went over there and was standing above him and he got right on up and I tell you I was riding that old buck through the woods . . . She's heard it all. The hunters bring in every conceivable form of meat. The first guy may have a whole deer shot that morning before going to work that he wants skinned and gutted and turned into breakfast sausage, roasted and sliced for po'boys, and the rest for tenderized steaks. The next may be a woman who showed up all the guys at deer camp and wants to get the head mounted by her son-in-law and have the meat ground for some green onion summer sausage, bacon burgers, and Cajun smoked sausage. It could be several hind-quarters brought in by some guys who got together and want hot tamales made of the whole lot. Teresa says, "Everything moves with a tag." The same cannot be said of some processing outfits. With the Milners you know it is your deer.

Watching Charlie break down a deer is something to see. He works deftly, slicing with graceful stokes while humming an uplifting tune. Rolling racks hold tubs with broken-down deer ranging in color from burgundy to pink as veal. A team of well-mannered young men stay on task, responding to orders with a "Yes, ma'am" or "Yes, sir," grinding each order, vacuum-sealing and labeling everything. A regular day can see thirty or forty deer brought in. Charlie works a day job for the Public Service Department, so things don't really crank up until after six in the evening and can go on until the wee hours of the morning. As fast as the deer come in, Teresa keeps them moving out. She gives you seven days to pick up your order. No exceptions. If after the call you are a no-show, the venison is sent as a donation to Mississippi Sportsmen Against Hunger and distributed to charities.

I have always enjoyed the taste of venison. Whitetails around here feed on wild Chickasaw plum, false indigo, clover, acorns, corn, and soybeans. I feel good about the meat. Handled properly, it has none of the "gamey" flavor folks shun. What it has is an earthiness of this place. The Milners' small business is part of what I enjoy about eating venison. I know they have handled the meat the way they would want someone to for them. They take care and pride in their work and their family.

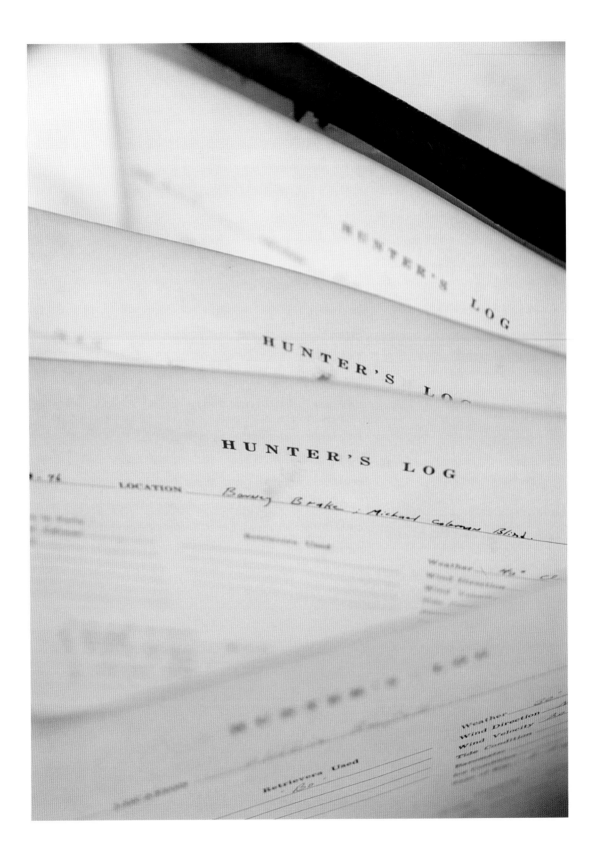

VENISON MEATBALLS
Silver Fox Mustard

Harry Van Heerden, my son's godmother's father, comes to visit each year from Durban, South Africa. Even at eighty-two, the silver-haired gent is quite a handful. When the sun starts to get low in the late afternoon he'll holler out "Vaapgae!" the Afrikaans word for "barrel." That's the cue to bring him a brandy.

Harry shared this mustard recipe with me and it does wonderful things for game, whether gemsbok or whitetail.

SERVES 6

2 large eggs

½ cup whole milk

1 cup fresh bread crumbs

½ cup grated Parmesan cheese

2 teaspoons chopped fresh parsley

1 teaspoon garlic powder

1 teaspoon salt

½ teaspoon freshly ground black pepper

1 pound ground venison

1 tablespoon olive oil

Silver Fox Mustard Sauce (recipe follows)

In a medium bowl, beat the eggs and milk. Add the bread crumbs, cheese, parsley, garlic powder, salt, and pepper; mix thoroughly. Add the venison and knead with your hands until well blended. Form into golf ball–size meatballs.

In a large skillet with a tight-fitting lid, heat the oil over medium-high heat. Add the meatballs and brown them on all sides, about 8 minutes. Add ½ cup of the mustard sauce, reduce the heat to low, and simmer, covered, for 30 minutes. Serve the meatballs with the remaining mustard sauce on the side.

NOTES

• This mustard sauce is very good on smoked meats and with summer sausage.

• If desired, keep half of the sauce as is and add 2 tablespoons prepared horseradish to the other half.

SILVER FOX MUSTARD SAUCE

MAKES ABOUT 1¼ CUPS

¼ cup dry mustard, preferably
    Colman's
1 (14-ounce) can sweetened
    condensed milk
½ cup white vinegar
1 tablespoon vegetable oil
1 teaspoon salt

In a small bowl, combine the mustard, condensed milk, vinegar, oil, and salt. Keep refrigerated for up to 1 month.

SODA CRACKERS
Toasty and Salty

I don't think people think of making their own crackers much, but homemade crackers can make store-bought dips and spreads set out for parties a little more personalized. A batch will last for a month stored in a tin and, when paired up with a hunk of good cheese, makes a very nice hostess gift.

MAKES 60 CRACKERS

4½ cups unbleached
    all-purpose flour
1 teaspoon baking soda
1 teaspoon fine sea salt, plus
    more for sprinkling
¾ cup lard or vegetable
    shortening, cold
2 cups whole milk

NOTES

- Add spices, seeds, or flavored salts to the top of these crackers as desired before baking.

- A funny colloquialism for someone not looking so good is "She looks like death eating a soda cracker." I don't know where it came from, but the women in my family have thrown it around for generations.

Heat the oven to 375°F.

In a large bowl, sift together the flour, baking soda, and salt. Cut in the lard until the mixture resembles coarse-cut oatmeal. Make a well in the center and add the milk. Toss with your hands and knead to form a stiff dough.

On a lightly floured work surface, roll out the dough until it is ⅛ inch thick. Cut into squares or whatever shape you desire. I like 1-inch squares or scalloped rounds. Prick the dough with the tines of a fork, brush lightly with water, and sprinkle with salt. Transfer to a baking sheet and bake for 20 minutes or until toasty and browned around the edges. Let cool before serving.

Salads, Soups & Dressings

Salsify Bisque—Oyster Plant

Pimiento Cheese Soup—With Grilled Bread

Green Pea Soup—With Broiled Salted Cream

New Potato and Spring Onion Soup—Rhythm of Spring

Dumpling Soup—Friendship Pagoda

Chicory Salad with Coffee Molasses Vinaigrette—Flower Clock

Dandelion Cracklings—Good Donny

Copper Pennies—Bride's Shoe

Potato and Anchovy Salad—Manly Salad

Plum Salad—Pretty Good

Winter Tangerine and Fennel Salad—Kid Gloves

Soybean Salad—Field of Dreams

Honey Pear Salad—Teddy Bear

Hominy Salad—Change the Station

Crab Ravigote—Sunday Service

Black and White Bean Salad—The Black and White Store, Yazoo City

Cranberry Salad—Thankfully

Alligator Pears and Bacon—Bite Me

Peanut Slaw—Ground Nuts

Feta Dressing—Greek Revival

SALSIFY BISQUE
Oyster Plant

Salsify is the root of a member of the sunflower family, although the plants—also called "goat's beard"—have a flower that looks more like a giant dandelion. The roots range from inky black to golden orange to turnip white. Salsify carries the nickname "oyster plant" due to its unique flavor, which has often been described as "oystery." I can't say I agree, but I do like it. The most popular variety grown for cooking is Mammoth Sandwich Island, which looks like a parsnip. "Scorzanera" is the Godfather-sounding name for black salsify. Both types can be used interchangeably in this recipe.

When working with salsify remember to treat it as you would an apple by placing it in water with a little lemon juice in it to keep the salsify from turning brown. Peel it just as you would a carrot, working near the sink, as it produces a milky sap that you will want to rinse off.

SERVES 6

1 pound salsify, peeled and
    chopped (about 2 cups)
½ cup chopped celery
1 tablespoon finely chopped
    onion
3 cups half-and-half
1 teaspoon salt
Sprinkle of cayenne pepper
2 large egg yolks, beaten
Grate of fresh nutmeg

NOTE
• Salsify has the nickname "viper's grass" and was thought to provide protection from snakebite.

In a large saucepan set over medium heat, cook the salsify, celery, and onion in the half-and-half until the mixture boils. Reduce the heat to low and add the salt and cayenne. Simmer for 10 minutes, stirring often, until the vegetables are tender.

Remove the pan from the heat. Using an immersion blender, or working in batches with a blender or food processor, blend until the mixture is almost smooth.

Add a small amount of hot bisque to the egg yolks and whisk to combine. Stir the yolk mixture into the soup. Return the pan to low heat and cook for 1 minute; do not boil. Serve immediately, with some nutmeg grated over the top.

PIMIENTO CHEESE SOUP
With Grilled Bread

Once bound by the southeastern borders, pimiento cheese has slowly swept the nation. This soup was just a matter of time. A big batch of this is perfect for Super Bowl parties and such.

SERVES 8

4 tablespoons (½ stick) unsalted butter

1 small white onion, finely chopped

3 celery stalks, leaves and all, finely chopped

⅔ cup unbleached all-purpose flour

5 cups chicken broth

1½ pounds extra-sharp Cheddar cheese, grated (5 cups)

1 quart half-and-half

2 (4-ounce) jars diced pimientos, rinsed and drained

1 teaspoon freshly ground black pepper

Salt

NOTE
• Serve this soup with bread that has been buttered and grilled on a grill pan until toasty.

In a large soup pot set over medium-low heat, cook the butter, onion, and celery for 6 minutes or until the onion turns translucent. Add the flour and stir until completely blended. Slowly add the broth, whisking until any lumps disappear. Turn the heat to low, then bit by bit stir in the cheese and half-and-half until the mixture is smooth. Add the pimientos and pepper, then season with salt. Cook, stirring often, for 10 minutes.

GREEN PEA SOUP
With Broiled Salted Cream

The peas, left whole, pop in your mouth with sweetness in each bite. The whipped salted cream browns underneath the broiler and blankets each spoonful with a froth.

SERVES 6

½ cup finely chopped carrots

½ cup finely chopped celery

½ cup finely chopped white onion

1 teaspoon dry mustard

½ teaspoon ground white pepper

1 pound frozen young green peas (or shelled fresh, of course, if you can get them)

1 cup heavy cream

1 teaspoon sea salt

NOTE

• Broiled paper-thin slices of ham are good served alongside like crackers. Ultra-thin-sliced Hillshire Farm smoked ham from the grocery works fine.

Pour 2 quarts water into a large saucepan. Add the carrots, celery, onion, mustard, and pepper. Bring the mixture to a boil over high heat, then reduce the heat and simmer for 45 minutes. Add the peas, bring the mixture back to a boil, and cook, stirring, for 3 minutes. Remove the pan from the heat. Scoop out ¾ cup of the cooked vegetables and set aside.

Return the pan to the heat and puree the soup with an immersion blender. Alternatively, you can puree the mixture in batches in a blender or food processor. Simmer the pureed soup for 30 minutes. Give the soup one more pass with the blender. Stir in the reserved vegetables.

Heat the broiler.

Whip the cream to form soft peaks. Ladle the soup into shallow ovenproof bowls and top with a big spoonful of whipped cream. Sprinkle some sea salt over the cream. Place the bowls under the broiler and broil for 2 minutes or until the cream browns slightly. Serve at once.

NEW POTATO AND
SPRING ONION SOUP
Rhythm of Spring

When I see the river rise and hear the birds sing, I think of my late dear friend Charlie Jacobs and his tune "Rhythm of Spring." His association between native produce and more innocent days elevates the memory of spring smells to a sort of romance. He beguiles us. And he tells us that from our soil comes the ingredient we need to find meaning. When I make this soup in the first cool days of spring, I'll serve it warm, and when the days begin to lengthen and turn warm, I like to serve it cool.

SERVES 8

3 tablespoons unsalted butter

4 spring onions, white and
   green parts, sliced

2 cups (½-inch) diced red new
   potatoes

6 cups chicken broth

1 cup crème fraîche

Salt and ground white pepper

NOTES
• Serve in teacups with a sprinkling of your
   favorite fresh herbs.

• If a smooth texture is desired, puree the soup
   while warm.

In a large saucepan set over medium heat, melt the butter and add the onions. Cook, stirring, for 2 minutes or until the green tops are tender. Add the potatoes and broth, raise the heat to medium-high, and bring to a boil. Reduce the heat to low and simmer, stirring occasionally, for 25 minutes or until the potatoes are tender.

Add a little of the warm soup to the crème fraîche, then stir the whole mixture into the soup. Taste and add salt and pepper as needed. Transfer to a storage container and let cool. Serve warm or chill in the refrigerator for at least 4 hours and serve cold.

DUMPLING SOUP
Friendship Pagoda

My favorite firework is the Friendship Pagoda. A little bright yellow house spins 'round like a top, emits sparks, and then up pops a pagoda and a little light glows within.

My son Joe's best first-grade friend is named Edison Seto. They make quite a pair. I love to see them out at recess walking with arms slung over each other's shoulder. Joe has had friends, of course, before first grade, but they were all friends of the family. Edison is the first friend he has made on his own. It looks as if Joe is a good judge of character, for Edison is as sweet as can be.

Edison lives in the family's New Sunlight Market with his parents, grandparents, and tiny sister, Grace. Joe loves to play over at Edison's. I would too; they get to ride their scooters up and down the aisles, snagging Little Debbie snack cakes for each lap.

Edison's family is from China and this has turned Joe into quite a fan of anything the slightest bit Chinese. This soup was inspired by their friendship and by the fine collard greens from the New Sunlight Market.

SERVES 6

6 cups chicken broth

2 cups cleaned and chopped collard greens

½ pound ground pork

¼ teaspoon grated peeled fresh ginger

1 tablespoon soy sauce

1 tablespoon toasted sesame oil

16 square wonton wrappers

¼ cup chopped green onions, white and green parts

Put the broth and collard greens in a large saucepan and set the pan over medium-high heat. Bring the mixture to a simmer.

Meanwhile, in a medium bowl, combine the pork, ginger, soy sauce, and sesame oil.

Arrange the wonton wrappers on a flat surface. Spoon the pork filling onto the center of each wrapper, to within ¼ inch of the edges (about 1 teaspoon per wrapper). With wet fingers, pinch the edges together to seal, forming a triangle. Then bring the side points together and press together.

NOTE
• Keep the stack of wonton wrappers covered with a barely damp towel when not working with them to keep them from drying. Also cover the finished wontons with a damp towel until ready to use.

Place the stuffed wontons into the slowly simmering broth. Cook for 8 minutes or until the wontons are tender and translucent. Remove the pot from the heat and stir in the green onions.

CHICORY SALAD WITH COFFEE MOLASSES VINAIGRETTE
Flower Clock

Chicory flowers are Aequinotales, meaning the flowers open and close at the same time just like clockwork. Here, that is from around six in the morning until the sun is high at noon. About the same time these blossoms are awakening, chicory roots blended with coffee are percolating across Louisiana. They make a fine combination. This dressing has the faintest sweetness of Louisiana molasses that works with the coffee to balance the bitter bite of the salad greens.

SERVES 4

⅓ cup balsamic vinegar

⅓ cup canola oil

¼ cup strong brewed coffee

¼ cup molasses

1 large egg (or 2 tablespoons egg substitute or pasteurized egg)

2 tablespoons powdered pectin (such as Sure-Jell)

1 garlic clove, chopped

½ teaspoon salt

¼ teaspoon red pepper flakes

2 small heads radicchio, leaves separated

2 heads Belgian endive, leaves separated

1 small head frisée, leaves separated

MAKE THE DRESSING. Combine ¼ cup water with the vinegar, oil, coffee, molasses, egg, pectin, garlic, salt, and red pepper flakes in a medium bowl. Whisk until combined. Store in the refrigerator until ready to use.

ASSEMBLE THE SALAD. Combine the radicchio, endive, and frisée in a large bowl. Add some of the dressing and toss to combine.

NOTES

• The addition of the pectin keeps the dressing from separating. You can store extra dressing in the refrigerator for up to 1 week. Another wonderful use for this dressing is to drizzle it over baked winter squash.

• Chicory, Belgian endive, and radicchio are varieties of *Cichorium intybus*. Endive and escarole are the plant *Cichorium endivia*.

• If planted in the right succession, Aequinotales can be used to make a flower clock. Carolus Linnaeus, a Swedish botanist, came up with a schedule of flowers around 1748 for his *Horologium Florae*.

DANDELION CRACKLINGS
Good Donny

What a nickname, Good Donny. It's a nickname most people couldn't live up to. His grandkids gave him that one and nobody has found grounds to disagree. Like the name implies, he's a good guy.

Good Donny's son, Benji, came by wielding some of the best pork cracklings we'd ever had. They were the perfect salty blend of tender, crisp, and crunch. Benji went on and on about how he had to beg Good Donny to give him just half a bag. Turns out that a friend of Good Donny's makes them and this friend is getting on up in age, meaning every batch might be the last. You would have thought Benji was passing out gold doubloons. Next time we saw Good Donny we made a point to tell him how crazy we were for those cracklings. The following day, Donny showed up with five pint bags full of those golden crispy treasures.

When Benji came by a few days later, my husband, Donald, retrieved a bag that he had hidden away. Benji was beside himself with envy.

SERVES 4

4 ounces young dandelion greens

2 thick slices bacon, chopped

3 tablespoons red wine vinegar

1 teaspoon cane syrup

½ teaspoon whole-grain mustard

Salt and freshly ground black pepper

4 large white mushrooms, sliced

2 tablespoons finely chopped red onion

2 hard-boiled eggs, chopped

1 cup pork cracklings

Remove the stems from the dandelion greens and wash the leaves, drain, and pat dry thoroughly. Put the greens in a large bowl and set aside.

In a small saucepan set over medium heat, fry the bacon until crisp. Transfer the bacon to a paper towel to drain, reserving 3 tablespoons of the rendered fat in the pan. Crumble the bacon and set aside.

Make a dressing by whisking the red wine vinegar, cane syrup, and mustard into the warm bacon drippings and season with salt and pepper.

NOTES

- Use very young crowns of dandelions; they become more bitter with age (like me).

- For an alternative version with a touch of sweetness, omit the egg and add 1 diced Granny Smith apple and 2 tablespoons chopped dried cranberries or pomegranate seeds.

Add the mushrooms and onion to the greens. Add the dressing and bacon and toss to combine. Divide the salad among 4 plates or bowls and evenly divide the egg among them. Sprinkle the top of each salad with cracklings.

COPPER PENNIES
Bride's Shoe

The rhyme that goes "something old, something new, something borrowed, something blue, and a silver sixpence in her shoe" has sent many a bride down the aisle. A sixpence is hard to come by these days, so many brides in these parts use a copper penny from the year they were born to help ensure a prosperous marriage, good luck, and protection against want. A few have a trinket for their charm bracelet made after the honeymoon.

Cutting carrots into rounds and marinating them in the dressing gives them a burnished look like copper pennies. It's nice to serve this at engagement parties celebrating a bride-elect.

SERVES 10

2 pounds carrots, sliced
1 cup sliced celery
2 onions, thinly sliced
1 green bell pepper, thinly
    sliced
1 (10-ounce) can tomato soup
⅔ cup sugar
⅔ cup cider vinegar
½ cup vegetable oil
1 teaspoon Worcestershire
    sauce
1 teaspoon Dijon mustard
1 teaspoon salt
½ teaspoon freshly ground
    black pepper

In a large pot, cook the carrots in boiling salted water until tender, about 5 minutes; do not over-cook. Drain well.

In a large bowl, combine the carrots, celery, onions, and bell pepper.

Combine the soup, sugar, vinegar, oil, Worcestershire, mustard, salt, and pepper in a pot. Heat over high heat until just boiling. Pour the hot mixture over the vegetables and stir to combine. Refrigerate for 12 hours before serving.

POTATO AND ANCHOVY SALAD
Manly Salad

This composed warm potato salad came together as a dish for my father. It has all the salty, tart flavors that he loves.

SERVES 6

1 pound small Yukon Gold or
    fingerling potatoes
1 (3-ounce) bottle capers,
    drained and liquid
    reserved
1 (2-ounce) can anchovies,
    drained and rinsed
1 tablespoon Dijon mustard
3 tablespoons red wine vinegar
½ cup extra-virgin olive oil
Freshly ground black pepper

In a large pot, cover the potatoes with salted water and bring to a boil. Cook for 20 minutes or until tender. Drain and set aside until cool enough to handle.

Cut the potatoes into ¼-inch-thick slices and arrange them on a serving platter. Scatter the capers and anchovies over the potato slices.

In a medium bowl, whisk together 1 tablespoon of the reserved liquid from the capers, the mustard, vinegar, and olive oil. Pour the dressing over the salad and grind pepper over the potatoes. Serve warm or chilled.

PLUM SALAD
Pretty Good

When something is really impressive, it is declared "plum good." As summer wears on and I grow tired of plum pies and tarts, I crave this simple, colorful salad. It is such a pretty mix of green and purple flecked with creamy white. The flavors offer sweet and sour, and the combination of textures—smooth, crunchy, and juicy—is really plum good. See photograph on page 5.

SERVES 6

4 plums, pitted and sliced into
    thin wedges
¼ cup pecan pieces, toasted
4 ounces crumbled blue
    cheese (1 cup)
⅓ cup extra-virgin olive oil
¼ cup balsamic vinegar
Salt and freshly ground black
    pepper
2 cups spinach leaves, torn
    into bite-size pieces

Combine the plums, pecans, blue cheese, olive oil, and vinegar in a large bowl. Season with salt and pepper and toss to combine. Chill for 1 hour.

Top the spinach with the plum and cheese mixture before serving.

NOTES

• Any stone fruit is wonderful substituted for or in conjunction with the plums.

• For plum trees to be at their best, produce the best fruit, and stay healthy, they need to be pruned right before spring. You must wait through the winter and see if any branches turn brittle and have to be removed. Around the middle of March is the time to cut them back. What one must remember is that fruits are produced from the horizontal branches, not the uprights. It's hard to cut those uprights off, but you must be brave; it's for y'all's own good.

• The first horizontal branches of fruit trees are called brave branches.

"What is more mortifying than to feel that you have missed the plum for want of courage to shake the tree?"
—LOGAN PEARSALL SMITH

WINTER TANGERINE
AND FENNEL SALAD
Kid Gloves

A tangerine, sometimes called "kid glove orange" because of the way its loose skin will slip off, has such a sweet, bright flavor when at its peak around November. This salad is fine-looking with light variegated shades of green set with vivid sections of citrus and golden challah croutons dusted with tarragon.

SERVES 6

CROUTONS

3 tablespoons unsalted butter

3 tablespoons vegetable oil

2 cups stale cubed challah or egg bread (left uncovered spread on a baking sheet overnight to dry)

2 tablespoons chopped fresh tarragon

1 teaspoon salt

½ teaspoon freshly ground black pepper

SALAD

1 fennel bulb, thinly sliced, fronds reserved

4 tangerines, peeled and sectioned (see Notes)

2 tablespoons fresh tangerine juice

2 tablespoons extra-virgin olive oil

1 teaspoon coarse sea salt

Freshly ground black pepper

MAKE THE CROUTONS. In a large skillet set over medium heat, melt the butter with the oil. Add the bread cubes and cook, stirring, for 5 minutes or until the bread is toasted. Sprinkle with the tarragon, salt, and pepper. Cool on a wire rack until needed or store in an airtight container for up to 3 days.

ASSEMBLE THE SALAD. Arrange the fennel and tangerine sections on a serving platter. Drizzle with the tangerine juice and olive oil, then sprinkle with the coarse salt and pepper. Top with the croutons and garnish with the fennel fronds.

NOTES

• To cut neat sections of citrus and remove the pith, use a very sharp paring knife and slice the skin off, removing as little flesh as possible. Then, over a bowl, cut along the divisions (between the membranes) with your knife, letting the sections fall in the bowl and catching the juice in the bowl too.

• A rite of passage for girls up until the sixties was to change from the little white cotton gloves girls wore to the white kid gloves of a young lady.

SOYBEAN SALAD
Field of Dreams

In 2009 the USDA declared seventy-nine of Mississippi's eighty-two counties disaster areas due to excessive rain in spring and fall and a drought in the summer. It rained more than fifteen inches in May when farmers were trying to plant their crops. Then in the busy harvest months, a deluge of eight inches in September, followed by fourteen and a half inches in October. It was one of the worst yields on record.

My cousin Michael Thompson has the right temperament to be a farmer. He is unflappable in the face of natural disaster and focuses on doing everything he can to foster a good soybean yield each season. "To do what I love on land that means so much to our family, it's home . . ." As he says this his voice trails off dreamily.

SERVES 4

2 medium cucumbers, peeled, quartered lengthwise, and cut into ¼-inch-thick slices

1 small onion, quartered and sliced

1 teaspoon kosher salt

1 cup cooked shelled edamame (soybeans)

3 tablespoons fresh lemon juice

2 tablespoons cottonseed or vegetable oil

½ teaspoon toasted sesame oil

1 tablespoon sesame seeds, toasted

¼ teaspoon cayenne pepper

Put the cucumber and onion slices in a bowl and toss with the salt. Allow to stand at room temperature for about 1 hour. Rinse, drain well in a colander, and return to the bowl.

Add the edamame, lemon juice, cottonseed oil, sesame oil, sesame seeds, and cayenne. Toss well to combine. Refrigerate for 30 minutes to allow the flavors to blend. Serve chilled or at room temperature.

HONEY PEAR SALAD
Teddy Bear

Holt Collier led the hunting expedition when Theodore Roosevelt visited Mississippi in 1902. The story goes that the president was desirous of a black bear to add to his trophy collection and was in a hurry to do so. Roosevelt was stationed in a blind, and Holt led chase to the elusive black bear with a pack of forty dogs. The impatient president left the stand to have lunch. With the success of the hunt resting on his shoulders, Holt took the initiative, captured the bear with a lariat, and tied it to a willow tree by the Little Sunflower River in an effort to save his dogs from the bear and fulfill the president's wishes. Moments later Roosevelt arrived on horseback and surveyed the scene. He declined to shoot a bear tied to a tree but was impressed by the bravery and abilities of Mr. Collier. The Washington Post *editorial cartoonist Clifford Kennedy Berryman ran two drawings on the front page of the paper of a cute little cub that in no way resembled the ferocious bear captured single-handedly by Collier.*

The story became a national sensation and an enterprising Morris Michtom sewed up a small stuffed bear cub and nicknamed it the Teddy Bear, selling them for a buck and a half each. By the next year Mr. Michtom had founded the Ideal Toy Company and was selling thousands of Teddies a year.

Today you can visit the first national refuge named for an African American, the 2,033-acre Holt Collier National Wildlife Refuge near Onward, Mississippi.

Each fall when the pears are ripe, the honey is in, and the Great Delta Bear Affair festival rolls around I think of that November hunt and that amazing American, Holt Collier.

SERVES 4

Nonstick cooking spray or
  unsalted butter

4 ripe pears, peeled, cored,
  and sliced

2 tablespoons honey

Grated zest and juice of
  1 lemon

½ teaspoon chopped fresh
  rosemary

½ cup diced country ham

¼ pound baby spinach

NOTE

• To learn more about the life of Holt Collier,
  check out Minor Ferris Buchannan's biography
  *Holt Collier: His Life, His Roosevelt Hunts, and
  the Origin of the Teddy Bear.*

Heat the oven to 375°F. Grease a small baking dish
with nonstick spray.

Put the pears into the prepared baking dish and add
the honey, lemon zest and juice, and rosemary. Toss
to combine. Bake for 10 minutes or until the honey
begins to bubble. Set aside to cool.

In a large bowl, combine the ham and spinach. Add
the pears and pan juices and toss to combine.

HOMINY SALAD
Change the Station

Hominy and tomatoes with a South Texas chili spice are a great change from boring potato salad. It is sort of like changing the radio dial from a typical oldies station to a fiesty, fun Mexican one.

SERVES 8

1 (14½-ounce) can golden hominy, rinsed and drained

1 (14½-ounce) can white hominy, rinsed and drained

2 cups chopped fresh tomatoes

¼ pound sharp Cheddar cheese, shredded (1 cup)

½ cup mayonnaise

¼ cup chopped green bell pepper

¼ cup chopped red bell pepper

4 green onions, white and green parts, chopped

2 tablespoons chopped fresh cilantro

1 teaspoon chili powder

1 teaspoon cumin seeds

1 teaspoon salt

Put the golden hominy, white hominy, tomatoes, cheese, mayonnaise, green bell pepper, red bell pepper, green onions, cilantro, chili powder, cumin seeds, and salt in a large bowl. Toss well to combine. Chill for at least 1 hour before serving.

NOTE
• The band Wall of Voodoo came out with a song called "Mexican Radio" when I was in high school. It was spicy and infectious and like nothing else on the radio at that time.

"This was due partly to habit and partly to affection born of a mixture of superiority and inferiority. . . . It was part of the Texas ritual. We're rich as son-of-a-bitch stew but look how homely we are, just as plain-folksy as Grandpappy back in 1836. We know about champagne and caviar but we talk hog and hominy."
—EDNA FERBER, FROM *GIANT*, A STORY SET IN TEXAS

CRAB RAVIGOTE
Sunday Service

Every year in early June Biloxi, Mississippi, holds the Blessing of the Fleet. Shrimp boats festooned with pennants, flags, as well as images of Jesus and animated shrimp form a procession out in the Mississippi Sound and file past the anchored "blessing boat." There stands the officiating priest, who sprinkles holy water on the boats and gives the blessing for each one. St. Michael's Catholic Church, with its stained-glass windows of Christ's twelve apostles depicted as fishermen and its scalloped roof, has been the central sponsor of the ceremony for more than eighty years. An evergreen wreath is dropped into the gulf in remembrance of those lost at sea, and prayers are offered up for a safe and prosperous fishing season. This year, with the oil spill, more than ever the fishermen could use a blessing.

This traditional coastal dish is perfect to serve for a Sunday brunch.

SERVES 8

2 large egg yolks

2 tablespoons fresh lemon
    juice

1 tablespoon white vinegar

2 teaspoons dry mustard

2 teaspoons Creole mustard

1 teaspoon prepared
    horseradish

1 teaspoon anchovy paste

⅓ teaspoon hot pepper sauce

1 teaspoon salt

1 cup vegetable oil

2 teaspoons Worcestershire
    sauce

4 hard-boiled eggs, grated

⅓ cup finely diced red bell
    pepper

Put the yolks, lemon juice, vinegar, dry mustard, Creole mustard, horseradish, anchovy paste, hot sauce, salt, and 1 tablespoon water in a medium bowl. Using an electric mixer, beat the mixture at high speed for 2 minutes. While the mixer is running, slowly drizzle in the oil to make a mayonnaise-like sauce. Stir in the Worcestershire, hard-boiled eggs, bell peppers, and green onions. Gently fold in the crabmeat.

Serve the mixture on top of the tomato slices and garnish with the caperberries.

⅓ cup finely diced yellow bell pepper

¼ cup thinly sliced green onions, white and green parts

2 (1-pound) cans lump crabmeat or 2 pounds cleaned fresh crabmeat

8 thick slices tomato

16 caperberries

NOTE
• This is wonderful served on an English muffin with a poached egg or on a bed of fine greens.

BLACK AND WHITE BEAN SALAD
The Black and White Store, Yazoo City

The Black and White Store down on the far west end of Main Street in Yazoo City opened the doors to its two-tone storefront in 1938. It stocks general merchandise and department-store goods; everyone in town shops there for fabrics and patterns, back-to-school clothes, new shoes, and footlockers for summer camp. Whenever I hear the words "black and white" I think of their big neon sign. Mr. Chisholm, the longtime manager, says at first the store was White's Store, with an aptly painted front; and when it expanded into the building next door that had been burned and the bricks charred black, it became the Black and White Store.

I was writing out a grocery list at home the other day and when I looked at the list at the store I had absentmindedly written "Black and White Store Beans" underneath "carrots." This salad ensued.

SERVES 6

1 (15-ounce) can black beans, rinsed and drained

1 (15-ounce) can Great Northern beans, rinsed and drained

2 carrots, grated

1 small green bell pepper, chopped

¼ cup finely chopped red onion

2 garlic cloves, minced

Grated zest and juice of 1 lime

¼ cup extra-virgin olive oil

1 teaspoon salt

1 teaspoon freshly ground black pepper

Put the black beans, Great Northern beans, carrots, bell pepper, onion, garlic, lime zest and juice, olive oil, salt, and pepper in a large bowl. Toss well to combine. Let the mixture stand for 1 hour before serving.

NOTE
• If it is summer and colorful bell peppers are cheap, add one in. If it's winter and they are $2.89 each, skip it.

Pageant Girls

There should be a contest—or, better yet, a pageant—of some sort. Some way to genuflect towards the spectacle of the congealed salad. I can picture it now. All those vibrant luncheon invitees lined up, each festooned with an array of garnishes (a sash would be nice for this occasion). Some demure in pink pastels of a chiffon nature, others a touch garish in light-diffracting lime green. Just like girls vying for a coveted tiara. Perennial favorites in attendance would surely include Blushing Peach Melba, Cherry Co-Cola Salad, Raspberry Ruby Pecan Salad, Carrot Pineapple Salad, and the otherworldly Jeweled Lime Surprise.

We know them or we know their type. Showing up (sometimes uninvited) to family reunions, backyard get-togethers, and potlucks. Some might look askance or offer a bemused smile when they see a congealed salad on a buffet (thinking to themselves one of my mother's favorite lines, "Oh, look what they like").

These "salads" (and sure, they might contain mini marshmallows, but I still will refer to them as salads), like pageant gals, don't just get thrown together. They come together over time and have very structured rules about what will do and what will not do. In pageants it seems padding, crossing your legs at the knee instead of the ankle, and smoking in the alley will not do. And no jiggling. In congealed salad making,

several rules apply too. No fresh papaya, ginger, mango, figs, pineapple, or honeydew can be used because the enzymes will keep the salad from setting up. Canned or poached versions, however, may be added, as the enzymes have been rendered inactive. Dumping a can of fruit cocktail into gelatin you are about to refrigerate is just making gelatin with fruit in it, not congealed salad. For things to stay mysteriously suspended, the additions must be gently folded in at just the right time—the moment when thickening has begun but coagulation has not occurred. The only way to get to this zen level of congealed salad making is to become a true devotee. I mean, those girls didn't just hop up there and start walking and waving. It took time and a great deal of study to get it down pat.

What I look for in a winning congealed salad is bright flavors and a combination of textures that you don't come across every day. Congealed salad (I am reserving thoughts on aspic for a later date) has gotten in with the kitschy kitchen set who rummage thrift shops for hostess aprons. With that "everything-old-is-new-again" enthusiasm that brought fondue back a few years ago, appearances of these triumphs of home economics are making a big comeback. Those from the hipster camp of molecular gastronomy have dubbed them "gelées" and don't even seem to be doing it with their tongues in their cheeks. That cranberry gelatin salad we all know has all but nixed out good old cranberry sauce on the holiday spread. I know it would be missed around these parts. Ambrosia gets the treatment from time to time and all sorts of congealed salad horizons avail themselves when cream cheese is stirred into the mix. What I guess I am trying to say is that congealed salads are not ironic. Silly? Yes. Ironic? No.

CRANBERRY SALAD
Thankfully

Thanksgiving Thursday starts off before dawn with Donald tiptoeing out of the house dressed in camouflage and with me making Aunt Mary's congealed salad of ground cranberries, apples, and navel oranges that I should have done the day before. (It's the recipe from the Tchula Garden Club Cookbook—except you would have to go across the road and get Mary's penciled-in revisions.) Instead, I sat by the fire drinking wine, catching up with extended family, and watched the kids pick up pecans. Now I'm hoping this sets before two o'clock dinnertime, which, thankfully, it does real nice.

SERVES 12

2 (3-ounce) packages
    raspberry gelatin

3 cups orange juice, heated

2 (¼-ounce) packages
    unflavored gelatin

1 tablespoon fresh lemon juice

1¼ cups sugar

3 cups fresh cranberries,
    washed and picked over

2 Granny Smith apples,
    peeled, cored, and cut
    into wedges

2 oranges, peeled and cut into
    bite-size pieces

1 (8-ounce) can crushed
    pineapple, with juice

¼ cup chopped pecans

Dissolve the raspberry gelatin in the hot orange juice in a large bowl. Soften the unflavored gelatin in ¼ cup cold water. Add to the raspberry gelatin along with the lemon juice and sugar and stir until well blended. Refrigerate until partially set, about 45 minutes.

Grind the cranberries and apples in a food processor until chopped fine. Add to the gelatin along with the oranges, pineapple and its juice, and nuts. Fold in to distribute. Pour into a 9 x 13-inch glass dish or gelatin mold and refrigerate until firmly congealed, about 2 hours.

NOTES

• Make sure you don't cut your apples too early; you don't want them to brown before you get the chance to stir them in.

• Serve slices of the salad with iceberg lettuce and homemade mayonnaise.

ALLIGATOR PEARS AND BACON
Bite Me

"Alligator pears" is what we call the big pale-skinned midwinter varieties of avocados. They're also known as Florida avocados (as opposed to the more familiar California Hass variety, which has dark, pebbly skin). One type has the name Bacon and that is a great coincidence since they work so wonderfully together.

SERVES 6

1 tablespoon extra-virgin olive oil

1 tablespoon red wine vinegar

Grated zest and juice of 1 lime

½ teaspoon salt

⅛ teaspoon red pepper flakes

Dash of hot pepper sauce, such as Tabasco

3 avocados, pitted, peeled, and diced

4 slices bacon, cooked and crumbled

1 large tomato, peeled, seeded, and diced

¼ cup finely chopped red onion

Whisk together the oil, vinegar, lime zest and juice, salt, red pepper flakes, and hot sauce. Put the avocados into a medium bowl, pour the dressing over them, and toss to combine. Stir in the bacon, tomato, and onion.

NOTE
• To ripen hard avocados, bury them in flour for a couple of days.

PEANUT SLAW
Ground Nuts

Like reverse butterflies, when the showy yellow blooms of peanuts begin to fade, the peduncle bows to the ground and buries its head in the earth, forming the webbed cocoon-like shells this legume is known for. This slaw is a great one for picnics in the hot summer because it isn't bound by mayonnaise. Chile, cilantro, and rice vinegar give it a fresh, spicy crunch that makes it the perfect peanutty partner for grilled chicken or pork.

SERVES 6

¼ cup peanut oil

2 tablespoons seasoned rice vinegar

1 teaspoon light brown sugar

2 teaspoons toasted sesame oil

2 teaspoons soy sauce

1 teaspoon hot chile sauce, such as Sriracha

½ large head napa cabbage, very finely chopped

½ cup thinly sliced green onions, white and green parts

1 bunch fresh cilantro, chopped

½ cup dry, unsalted roasted peanuts, chopped

Salt and freshly ground black pepper

NOTE
• This is very good with Peanut Chicken (page 174).

In a bowl or glass measuring cup, mix together the peanut oil, rice vinegar, brown sugar, sesame oil, soy sauce, and chile sauce. Whisk together until the dressing is well combined.

In large plastic bag or glass bowl, gently combine the cabbage, green onions, and cilantro. Add the dressing and chopped peanuts, season with salt and pepper, and stir a few times until the peanuts are mixed in.

FETA DRESSING
Greek Revival

When you say "Greek" in Oxford, Mississippi, most people will think you are talking about one of three things: sororities and fraternities, antebellum architecture, or Angelo Mistolis's feta cheese salad dressing. This dressing of mine is great on cold-cut foot-longs and on salads of all sorts.

MAKES 1½ CUPS

¼ pound feta cheese, crumbled (1 cup)

1½ cups vegetable oil

½ cup white vinegar

¼ cup grated white onion

2 tablespoons capers, drained and chopped

2 garlic cloves, minced

1 teaspoon ground white pepper

½ teaspoon dried oregano

½ teaspoon salt

Combine the feta, oil, vinegar, onion, capers, garlic, pepper, oregano, and salt in a container with a lid and shake like crazy.

NOTES
• For gift giving, I like to pour the dressing into a Mason jar. Since the recipe makes 1½ cups, it is enough for one half-pint to give—and some to keep for myself!

Vegetables & Grains

Jerusalem Artichokes—Holy Land

Asparagus with Country-Ham-and-Egg Gravy—Spring

Italian Green Beans—Romanos

Creamed Onions—Egyptian Walking Onions

Sugar Snap Peas—Peaches Please

Sugarcane Sweet Potatoes—Evangeline and Emmeline

Skillet Fried Corn—Off the Cob

Corn "Oysters"—Po'boy?

Baked Pumpkin—Funny Face

Grilled Green Onions—Korean Barbecue

Glazed Rutabagas—Jule's Jewels

Crisp Tender Potatoes—Both

Do the Mashed Potatoes—James Brown and the Famous Flames

Bamboo Shoots with Black Bean Sauce—First Acre

Deviled Tomatoes—Spicy Cindy

Tomatoes in Leaves—Last of the Season

Pigeon Peas and Rice—Back in the Kitchen

Indian Green Peas with Paneer—An Arranged Marriage

Sweet and Sour Salsify—Unique

Squash Blossoms—Full Bloom

JERUSALEM ARTICHOKES
Holy Land

The Palestine Gardens is a miniature replica of sites from the Holy Land built down in the piney woods around Lucedale, Mississippi. For sixteen years Reverend Walter Harvell Jackson and his wife searched for a place to build his Bible-themed garden. After seven years of construction, the forty-acre garden opened in 1960 with Bethlehem, Jericho, and Jerusalem all constructed out of concrete blocks, and with its own Dead Sea. It has expanded over the years to include the Sea of Galilee.

Jerusalem artichokes do well in the kind of sandy soil and full sun they have down there in George County and will thrive in most gardens, producing the edible tubers and brilliant yellow sunflowers. I like to serve this over Israeli couscous, of course.

SERVES 4

1 lemon, halved

1½ pounds Jerusalem
    artichokes

2 tablespoons olive oil

2 garlic cloves

Sprig of fresh thyme

1 teaspoon salt

¼ teaspoon freshly ground
    black pepper

Squeeze the lemon into a bowl of water. Thinly slice the lemon and set the slices aside.

With a sharp knife, scrape the outside skin of the artichokes just to remove the dark nubs. Slice the artichokes into ¼-inch slices and put them in the bowl of lemon water.

In a large skillet set over medium-low heat, heat the oil. Drain the artichoke slices and put them in the skillet. Add the lemon slices, garlic, and thyme. Season with the salt and pepper. Cook, stirring, for 10 minutes or until the artichokes are tender when pierced with a knife.

NOTE
• Jerusalem artichokes are also called sunchokes.

ASPARAGUS WITH COUNTRY-HAM-AND-EGG GRAVY
Spring

Spring is a short-lived but well-loved season in the Mississippi Delta. All is verdant and lush with the scent of fresh-tilled earth in the air. When spears of asparagus are combined with farm-fresh eggs, to me, it all signals spring. I particularly enjoy this dish for breakfast with sourdough bread for sopping up the luxuriant, velvety cream sauce.

SERVES 4

1 pound asparagus, trimmed
½ cup diced country ham
2 tablespoons unsalted butter
2 tablespoons unbleached all-purpose flour
2 cups whole milk
2 hard-boiled eggs, chopped
½ teaspoon salt
Freshly ground black pepper
Chopped fresh dill or chive blossoms, for garnish

Blanch the asparagus in boiling salted water for 2 minutes and drain.

In a medium saucepan set over low heat, cook the ham in the butter for 5 minutes. Sprinkle the flour over the ham and cook, stirring, for 1 minute. Raise the heat to medium and slowly add the milk while stirring constantly. Cook, stirring, for 2 minutes or until the sauce has thickened and begins to bubble. Remove the pan from the heat and stir in the chopped egg, salt, and pepper.

Arrange the asparagus on a serving platter and spoon the ham-and-egg sauce over the top. Garnish with fresh dill.

NOTE
• This is one I seem to serve that Monday after Easter Sunday, when these ingredients are hanging around and the dish can be made with leftovers.

ITALIAN GREEN BEANS
Romanos

Romano beans (aka Italian string beans) are really just a different variety of snap bean, and are grown and eaten the same way. Broad flat-podded green snap beans with five- to six-inch pods are often called Italian Pole or Romano beans, and varieties include Roma, Greencrop, and Bush Romano.

Anchovy paste makes these good; don't tell folks what is in them and they will eat them up.

SERVES 4

1 pound fresh Italian green
    beans, cut into ½-inch
    pieces
3 garlic cloves, chopped
3 tablespoons olive oil
1 teaspoon anchovy paste
Freshly ground black pepper
2 ounces Romano cheese,
    shaved with a vegetable
    peeler

In a large skillet set over medium heat, cook the green beans and garlic in the olive oil for 2 minutes. Add ½ cup water to the pan. Cook, stirring, for 10 minutes or until the beans are tender. Stir in the anchovy paste and pepper.

Using a slotted spoon or tongs, transfer the green beans to a serving platter and top with the Romano cheese.

CREAMED ONIONS
Egyptian Walking Onions

Egyptian walking onions do just that; they walk their way across a garden. These unusual plants produce clusters of onion sets at the top of their stalks. As the sets at the top mature and become too heavy for the stalks to hold them upright, they lean over to the ground and replant themselves, traveling across the yard. When the new sets are buried, a petite onion will form. Once these are established they will travel, producing onions along the way, for years. The onions harvested from walking onions are very similar to pearl onions and, like their cousins, are delicious creamed. See photograph on page 106.

SERVES 2

¾ pound Egyptian walking onions or pearl onions, peeled (see Notes)

⅔ cup heavy cream

1 garlic clove, minced

½ teaspoon salt

1 tablespoon unsalted butter

Dash of hot pepper sauce

Grate of fresh nutmeg

Freshly ground black pepper

Heat the oven to 350°F.

Combine the onions, cream, garlic, and salt in a small baking dish. Dot the top with the butter and add a little hot sauce, nutmeg, and pepper. Bake for 25 minutes or until the onions are beginning to brown and are very tender.

NOTES
- To peel pearl onions, cut off a small bit of root end from each onion and drop the onions in boiling water. Let boil for 3 minutes, then submerge in cold water. The peels will slip off easily.

- If you like, add ½ cup blanched almonds to the onions as Helen Corbitt did.

- One of my favorite Southern authors is Clyde Edgerton, who wrote a novel called *Walking Across Egypt*. The title comes from one of the lead character's favorite hymns, which was written by Mr. Edgerton himself!

"A good cook will, no doubt, approach the pearly gates with an onion in one hand and a pound of butter in the other."
—*HELEN CORBITT'S COOKBOOK* 1957

SUGAR SNAP PEAS
Peaches Please

The sweetness of peaches and sugar snap peas makes them pair up quite well. A bit of seasoning sends the duo down a chutney path.

SERVES 4

½ cup chopped peeled fresh peaches

1 tablespoon cider vinegar

1 tablespoon chopped yellow onion

1 tablespoon golden raisins

½ teaspoon grated peeled fresh ginger

1 teaspoon cane syrup

½ teaspoon grated lemon zest

1 garlic clove, minced

¼ teaspoon mustard seeds

⅛ teaspoon red pepper flakes

Pinch of ground cinnamon

Pinch of ground cloves

Pinch of ground allspice

4 cups sugar snap peas (1 pound), trimmed

Combine the peaches, vinegar, onion, raisins, ginger, cane syrup, lemon zest, garlic, mustard seeds, red pepper flakes, cinnamon, cloves, and allspice in a large bowl. Cover and microwave on high for 1 minute. Add the peas, cover, and cook on high for 2 minutes or until the peas are tender.

SUGARCANE SWEET POTATOES
Evangeline and Emmeline

I was a boy-crazy preteen when I went on a trip to visit my friend's grandmother Beauxma in Saint Martinville, Louisiana, in the sugarcane-growing region of the state. I was so taken by the story of the Evangeline Oak.

In 1907, St. Martinville author Felix Voorhies wrote Acadian Reminiscences: With the True Story of Evangeline, *inspired by tales told to him by his grandmother. The account of Emmeline Labiche and Louis Arceneaux is said to be about the real people behind Longfellow's tragically romantic poem "Evangeline," about a woman looking for her lost love, Gabriel.*

In 1929, Hollywood came to town and filmed the movie Evangeline, *starring Dolores Del Rio in the title role. After the filming, a statue of Evangeline (looking a lot like Dolores Del Rio) was erected on the spot marking the alleged burial place of Emmeline Labiche.*

As a whole, Southerners have never let the truth stand in the way of a good story; and now the stories of Emmeline and Louis and Evangeline and Gabriel have fused into one story told time and again beneath the spreading branches of the Evangeline Oak. In fact, Louisianans have taken the story so to heart that the Evangeline variety of sweet potato is fast becoming one of the state's most popular sweet potatoes.

NOTE
• Sugarcane skewers are strips of sugarcane and can be used for kebabs or swizzle sticks. Look for them in the produce section or in ethnic markets or online.

SERVES 8

1½ pounds sweet potatoes, peeled and cut into 2-inch chunks

3 tablespoons olive oil

2 tablespoons chopped fresh parsley

¼ teaspoon ground chipotle powder or cayenne pepper

Salt and freshly ground black pepper

1 red bell pepper, cut into 2-inch chunks

1 green bell pepper, cut into 2-inch chunks

1 cup pineapple chunks

8 (8- to 10-inch) metal or wooden skewers or sugarcane skewers (see Note)

Heat a grill to medium-high.

Put the potato chunks in a microwave-safe 2-quart baking dish and add ½ cup water. Cover and microwave for 5 to 10 minutes, until the potatoes are firm-tender (do not overcook or they will be too mushy to grill). Drain the potatoes.

In a small bowl, whisk together the oil, parsley, chipotle powder, salt, and black pepper. Pour the mixture over the potatoes and stir to coat. Alternate threading the potatoes, bell peppers, and pineapple chunks onto the skewers.

Grill the kebabs, turning frequently, for 15 minutes, or until a nice brown crust forms.

Sweet Corn

Used to be, in the Mississippi Delta, the only corn you saw growing was in someone's home garden. Sometimes you'd catch a glance of an acre or so that somebody had planted with visions of filling their carport Sears chest freezer with homegrown sweet corn still on the cob or bags stuffed with shorn pegs, almost ready for the Sunday dinner table. But for the most part, in the flatlands of Mississippi, growing sweet corn was sort of a gardening folly.

Sweet corn is very particular about how it grows. You might go so far as calling it persnickety. Corn likes rich soil, which of course we have, but it also likes even moisture. And as anyone who has spent time in my part of the world will tell you—except for the ever-present humidity in the air— moisture is just not something you can count on. So while all farming is a gamble, growing corn in the Mississippi Delta comes with especially high risks. Yet if those risks pay off, man, do you ever have some good eating.

So Delta folks have continued optimistically and somewhat successfully to grow corn—three basic kinds—in home gardens. There is the supersweet variety that has small kernels and tastes really good, but it's hard to get started in the garden and can cause a lot of heartache before you even get to the tasting part. This kind of corn has up to three times the sugar found in other sweet corn varieties. There is also a sugar-enhanced variety that has a creamier taste, and then there is the normal sweet corn with kernels that are yellow, white, or bicolored.

Somewhere over the last decade farming practices in the Delta shifted. Demand for cotton dropped, and so did the prices. At the same time, demand and prices for corn escalated. So travelers driving down a Mississippi highway today are more likely to see acre after acre of corn rather than the expected crops of cotton and soybeans. It's something that we are still getting used to, and the *New York Times* even ran a story about how the Mississippi farming landscape has changed to the point where we are beginning to look like Iowa. This is weird to us, seeing all that corn around.

I'm a cook, not a farmer. So it's out of my range of expertise to determine a variety of corn from a passing vehicle. In my head, I live in a land of lemonade rivers, houses of moist gingerbread, and boulders of rock candy. So in my mind, all corn is sweet corn. So now that the Delta is home to thousands of acres of cornfields, everywhere I turn I'm presented with visions of kernels waiting to pop in my mouth like some sort of filled Christmas candy, leaving the corners of my mouth glistening with wayward melted butter and depositing sweet, tiny remains between my teeth that require a torn corner of a matchbook to dislodge. In my mind, none of the corn I see growing around Pluto ends up as cattle feed or biodiesel or—God forbid—the world's greatest kitty litter. Yellow or white, commercially grown or nurtured in a tiny garden plot, ten ears to a stalk or one single giant cob, it is always sweet corn.

Coming of age here, a child is not considered socialized until he or she can independently hold a barbecued spare rib or a cob of sweet corn. When you reach an age where you can sit up straight in your grandmother's highchair and suck on one of these two items without listing, you are officially a member of the family—if not polite society. Southern mothers don't worry about infants choking on an ear of sweet corn because, let's face it: If you only have two teeth, you can't get much more than the juice out of a kernel anyway. So down here, kids of a certain age are handed a buttery piece of sweet corn and pretty much turned loose and ignored while the adults get down to the serious business of tearing every single kernel off their own cob—and, if they are smart—sucking on what's left afterward just to be sure nothing was missed.

No state fair worth its mettle can afford not to offer corn hot off a charcoal grill, stripped of its silk, husks folded back, then dipped in Phase Liquid Butter Alternative (I know it comes as a shock, people, but that's *not* real butter). It's a rite of passage to walk hand in hand with your date past the Tilt-A-Whirl while gnawing on an ear of sweet corn with your free hand. Some Southern cafés deep fry frozen corn on the cob and serve it up on waxed paper in red-and-white plaid paper boats with a hefty sprinkling of salt. Frying makes the kernels a little leathery and tougher to get off the cob, but it seems to enhance the sweetness of the juice, which makes the extra chewing worthwhile.

You'll find a few Delta cooks who make creamed corn, but historically this is not a part of our culinary canon. Milk—and especially whole cream—has traditionally been considered a luxury in rural areas such as the Delta. So creamed corn is really more of a Midwestern fare, served in places where there are plenty of not only cornfields but also cows and, thus, dairy products.

Lacking readily available fresh dairy items, we in the Delta turn to the next creamiest ingredient we have on hand: bacon fat or lard. Now, before anyone starts talking about how unhealthy bacon fat or lard is, go research whole cream. Then get back to me. In the meantime, I'll be thinking about how freshly shorn sweet-corn kernels folded into a cast-iron skillet holding hot bacon fat just itching to pop with the slightest touch of moisture will produce one of the most delectable Southern courses found on any table.

Like many of the best dishes from the Delta, skillet-fried sweet corn is made from ingredients already hanging around in the kitchen. The bacon fat is scooped from an ever-present jar kept on the back of the stove. The salt and pepper are found in dented aluminum shakers with handles and sitting on either side of the drippings container. The garlic is grown right outside the kitchen door, where it's not only handy for cooking but it looks really pretty, too.

The only ingredient that's ever iffy is the corn, and we're about to get that down too.

SKILLET FRIED CORN
Off the Cob

When Ernestine Williams, mother of Ole Miss Colonel Reb and NFL football great Gentle Ben Williams, was teaching me how to make skillet fried corn, the top of the black pepper shaker fell off and a ton of pepper fell in the skillet. She scooped out as much as she could but there was still a whole lot that got left in. We liked it. Now when I make it I add a good bit of black pepper and a whole lot of garlic. You have to use fresh corn in this dish; frozen just won't do if you want it to really fry up nice.

SERVES 6

8 ears fresh corn, kernels cut off
2 tablespoons unsalted butter
1 tablespoon lard or bacon grease
4 garlic cloves, chopped
Salt and freshly ground black pepper

In a large skillet set over high heat, cook the corn in the butter and lard for 4 minutes or until it begins to brown. Add the garlic, season heavily with salt and pepper, and cook for 1 minute.

NOTE

• An angel food cake pan is just the right thing to employ when cutting corn off the cob. Stand the corn right up on the tube and let the kernels fall into the pan! My Facebook friend Christy Jordan taught me that trick.

CORN "OYSTERS"
Po'boy?

Fry these up and stuff them in a big roll with shaved cabbage and mayo for your vegetarian friends. They deserve big po'boys of fried things too! Or serve them as a side or even a party-food popper.

SERVES 6

2 large eggs, separated
½ teaspoon dark brown sugar
1¼ teaspoons salt
6 ears fresh corn, kernels cut from the cobs (3 cups; see Note, page 121)
2 tablespoons buttermilk
½ cup unbleached all-purpose flour
½ cup cornmeal
2 teaspoons baking powder
Vegetable oil, for frying

In a bowl, whisk together the egg yolks, brown sugar, and ½ teaspoon of the salt until the mixture is pale and slightly thickened. Put the corn in a large bowl. Add the buttermilk and the egg-yolk mixture and stir to combine

Whisk together the flour, cornmeal, baking powder, and the remaining ¾ teaspoon salt. Stir into the corn until just combined.

Heat 2 inches of oil in a large pot or electric skillet to 325°F.

Beat the egg whites until medium to stiff peaks form. Fold the whites into the corn mixture until thoroughly combined.

Working in batches, drop the corn mixture into the hot oil 1 tablespoon at a time. Fry on one side for 2 to 3 minutes, until golden. Turn the fritters and fry the second side for 2 minutes or until golden. Remove and drain on a wire rack set over a paper-towel-lined baking sheet to catch drips.

BAKED PUMPKIN
Funny Face

Jack-o'-lanterns are wonderful. When else does a vegetable get to have so much fun?
Serve this roasted pumpkin with the lights down dim and tell the spooky story of Stingy
Jack tricking the devil once you get home from trick-or-treating.

SERVES 4

1 small sugar pumpkin (about
    3 pounds)
2 tablespoons unsalted butter,
    melted
2 tablespoons pure maple
    syrup
2 teaspoons flaky sea salt

NOTE
• If you want, carve a crazy face in it when
  serving just as you would when making a
  jack-o'-lantern.

Set an oven rack in the lowest position and heat the oven to 350°F. Line a roasting pan with parchment paper or foil.

Cut off the top of the pumpkin and scrape out all the seeds. Put the butter and maple syrup inside the pumpkin and, using a pastry brush, coat the inside flesh; sprinkle with the salt. Put the pumpkin lid back on and put the pumpkin in the prepared pan. Pour in enough water to come ½ inch up the side of the pumpkin. Bake for 40 minutes or until tender.

Remove the pumpkin from the baking dish to a platter. Cut the pumpkin into serving pieces.

GRILLED GREEN ONIONS
Korean Barbecue

My cousin Daniel Foose fell in love with a girl he met in music school. Sueyoung Yoo and Daniel married out at our family farm, Pluto, on what might have been the hottest day that year, Saturday, June 30. Friends and family began to arrive the Wednesday before. As the bride and groom are both accomplished jazz musicians, she a pianist and he a bassist, most of the bridal party came with instruments in tow, and late-night jams filled the evenings.

Sueyoung made kimchi, massaging each leaf of cabbage with rich chile paste and placing it in her groom's great-grandmother's soup tureen. Her soon-to-be in-laws, Uncle Jon and Aunt Caroline, had driven from Austin with a plug-in home-size chest freezer in the back of their Suburban rigged to a battery and filled with all sorts of slow-cooked Creole and Tex-Mex food for the reception. The reception came together in an eccentric perfection combining cooking from New Orleans, Korea, Mississippi, and Texas; and the band played well into the night.

It is a joy to have Sueyoung in the family. Now out at Pluto we have kimchi buried in the yard and Korean barbecue is served on Christmas night.

SERVES 6

4 bunches green onions or
    purple scallions
1 tablespoon sugar
1 small garlic clove, minced
¼ cup soy sauce
¼ cup sake
1 tablespoon honey
½ cup finely chopped Asian
    pear or Golden Delicious
    apple

Heat the grill to low.

In a food processor, pulse together the white part of one of the green onions with the sugar, garlic, soy sauce, sake, honey, and pear.

Place the remaining green onions on the grill 4 to 6 inches above low coals or over low flame and brush them with the soy sauce mixture. Cook for 5 minutes, turning as needed, or until the onions are tender. Remove from the heat and brush with more sauce right before serving.

GLAZED RUTABAGAS
Jule's Jewels

These glazed rutabagas look like topaz when cooked down with brown sugar, cider vinegar, and butter. My friend Jule adores rutabagas and thrift store jewelry. I came up with this dish for her.

SERVES 6

1 large rutabaga (about 2 pounds), peeled and cut in ½-inch dice
2 tablespoons unsalted butter
2 tablespoons dark brown sugar
1 tablespoon cider vinegar
1 teaspoon salt

Put the rutabaga in a large skillet and add enough salted water to cover. Set over medium-high heat and bring to a simmer. Cook for 10 minutes or until slightly tender. Drain off the water and add the butter, brown sugar, vinegar, and salt. Bring to a boil, reduce the heat to low, and simmer for 12 minutes or until the rutabaga is very tender and the butter begins to brown. Serve warm.

CRISP TENDER POTATOES
Both

My in-laws grew up in Indiana. My husband grew up in a meat-and-potatoes type of home. This changeable delectable potato dish can match up with anything. The potatoes inside are tender and flavored with the broth and the potatoes on top are nicely crisped and browned.

SERVES 6

2 pounds russet potatoes, peeled and very thinly sliced

3 tablespoons olive oil

2 medium onions, very thinly sliced

Salt and freshly ground black pepper

1¼ cups vegetable broth

⅔ cup whole milk

Soak the potato slices in cold water for 30 minutes. Drain, rinse, and pat dry.

Heat the oven to 350°F.

Drizzle 1 tablespoon of the oil in the bottom of a 9 x 13-inch baking dish. Alternately layer the potatoes and onions, seasoning with salt and pepper between the layers. Drizzle the remaining 2 tablespoons oil over the top. Pour in the broth and milk. Bake on the top rack of the oven for 50 minutes or until the potatoes can be pierced easily with a fork and the top is brown and crisp.

NOTE
• Add your favorite sturdy herb to the potatoes, such as rosemary or thyme. If pairing with meat, use the appropriate broth.

DO THE MASHED POTATOES
James Brown and the Famous Flames

The dance the Mashed Potato was all the rage after James Brown incorporated it into his rousing live show and review with his band the Famous Flames. Under a contract with a recording label that did not think much of the idea, in 1959 Brown took the song down to a friend's studio in Florida and recorded the hit song "(Do the) Mashed Potato."

So he would not run afoul of his own label, Brown billed the song as Nat Kendrick and the Swans and the lyrics were attributed to one of Brown's aliases, Dessie Rozier. Soon the nation was whipped up in the craze with two other hit songs, "Mashed Potatoes U.S.A." and "The Mash Potato Man."

It is fun to use purple potatoes the same color as James Brown's famous cape to make mashed potatoes while having a kitchen dance party with the kids.

SERVES 4

1½ pounds purple sweet
    potatoes (see Note),
    peeled
Salt
½ cup whole milk
2 tablespoons unsalted butter
½ teaspoon ground white
    pepper

NOTE
• Purple sweet potatoes are grown in Stokes County, North Carolina. If you can't find sweet potatoes, use a purple variety of potato. It won't be sweet—it's all about the color.

Put the potatoes in a medium saucepan and cover them with water. Salt the water generously. Bring to a boil and simmer for 15 minutes or until the potatoes are tender but not mushy.

Meanwhile, combine the milk and butter in a small saucepan set over medium-low heat. Bring to a simmer and remove from the heat.

Drain the potatoes, return them to the pan, and set the pan over low heat for 1 minute to dry the potatoes out. Remove the pan from the heat and mash the potatoes with a potato masher or fork while gradually adding the warm milk mixture. Season with salt and pepper.

BAMBOO SHOOTS
WITH BLACK BEAN SAUCE
First Acre

Cousin Louis and my father have become bamboo enthusiasts. Louis has planted his first acre of black bamboo to see how it does as a field crop. It is used as an ornamental and in several developing fiber markets. My father even ordered a special bamboo saw from Japan to trim his ever-expanding collection of bamboo varieties.

Bamboo shoots are edible and it is a once-a-year treat to get them freshly sprouted. You can also find fresh bamboo shoots in many Asian markets and specialty produce stands. The ones on the grocery shelf are always at the ready year-round.

SERVES 4

⅔ cup chicken broth

2 tablespoons fermented black beans, rinsed and mashed

2 garlic cloves, minced

1 tablespoon soy sauce

1 teaspoon oyster sauce

2 teaspoons cornstarch

1 teaspoon sugar

1 tablespoon peanut oil

2 cups peeled and thinly sliced with the grain prepared fresh bamboo shoots (about 3; see Note), or 4 (4-ounce) cans bamboo shoots, rinsed and drained

Combine the broth, black beans, garlic, soy sauce, oyster sauce, cornstarch, and sugar in a small saucepan set over medium-high heat. Bring the mixture to a boil. Cook, stirring, for 1 minute. Remove from the heat and set aside.

Heat a medium skillet over medium heat until hot. Add the oil and bamboo shoots. Cook, stirring, for 3 minutes or until the shoots are tender. Pour the sauce over the bamboo shoots and toss to coat. Serve at once.

NOTE

• If fresh bamboo tastes very bitter, blanch it in salted water for 2 minutes, cool in cold water, then drain, and carry on.

DEVILED TOMATOES
Spicy Cindy

My friend Cindy Nix Sturdivant lives on the Countiss Place near Swan Lake, Mississippi. She has a nice plot of tomatoes, herbs, and peppers out the back door of her kitchen. This hot and spicy dish is inspired by her. She is so much fun because she can always get folks fired up for a party, like her epic dove hunt party, which grows every year, on Labor Day weekend. She needs to plant a bigger plot.

SERVES 6

6 slices bacon, cut in ½-inch pieces

1 cup chopped green bell pepper

1 cup chopped red onion

2 jalapeño peppers, seeded and diced

2 garlic cloves, minced

3 large tomatoes, peeled and halved

1 tablespoon chopped fresh oregano

Salt and freshly ground black pepper

6 slices sourdough bread, toasted

¼ pound pepper Jack cheese, shredded (½ cup)

NOTE
• Nix [no relation to Cindy] vs. Hedden was the case that brought the question of whether a tomato is a fruit or a vegetable before the U.S. Supreme Court in 1893. Although the tomato is a fruit, the court unanimously ruled that the tomato would be thought of as a vegetable in regards to the Tariff Act of 1883, setting a precedent that still holds today.

In a large skillet set over medium heat, cook the bacon until crisp, about 6 minutes. Transfer the bacon to paper towels and reserve the bacon drippings in the pan. Add the bell pepper, onion, jalapeños, and garlic to the pan. Cook, stirring occasionally, for 5 minutes.

Meanwhile, scoop the flesh out of the center of the tomatoes and chop, reserving the shells. Add the chopped flesh to the pan. Stir in the oregano, season with salt and pepper, and cook for 2 minutes.

Place an oven rack in the center of the oven and heat the broiler.

Put the bread slices in a 9 x 13-inch baking dish. Top each slice of bread with a tomato half. Divide the vegetable mixture evenly among the tomato halves. Top each with cheese. Broil for 3 minutes or until the cheese is melted.

TOMATOES IN LEAVES
Last of the Season

Peeking out from dried leaves, last-of-the-season tomatoes can be some of the most flavorful. Here they are wrapped in leaves of phyllo pastry and baked with just a bit of Dijon mustard.

SERVES 6

6 small very ripe tomatoes

10 fresh phyllo pastry sheets, or frozen, thawed (each sheet about 17 x 13 inches)

10 tablespoons (1¼ sticks) salted butter, melted, plus more for the pan

6 teaspoons Dijon mustard

NOTES

• You can vary the size of muffin cups and phyllo squares to match your tomatoes, from mini muffin pans to fit cherry toms to jumbo muffin tins to fit larger varieties. For cherry or pear tomatoes, use a mini muffin pan with 2½- to 3-inch slots and cut 4-inch squares of phyllo. For plum and Roma tomatoes, use a muffin tin with 4-inch slots and cut 5-inch squares. For larger tomatoes, use a muffin pan with 5-inch slots and cut 6-inch squares.

• Arkansas Traveler, Marion, and Mule Team are varieties of tomatoes grown in Mississippi.

Heat the oven to 375°F. Generously butter every other cup in a 12-cup muffin pan.

Cut off the stem end of each tomato so that it will stand up cut side down. Set aside.

Brush one sheet of phyllo dough with melted butter and stack another on top. Continue, brushing each sheet with melted butter, until 5 sheets are stacked. Cut squares from the buttered sheets (see Notes).

Place the squares of dough in the buttered cups, pressing firmly against the sides and bottom of the pan and leaving the corners sticking up.

Place 1 teaspoon mustard in each cup, then add a tomato, cut side down. Bake for 10 minutes or until the phyllo is crisp and brown.

PIGEON PEAS AND RICE
Back in the Kitchen

I like the browned bits that cling to the skillet, like the socarrat of a paella, when I cook this side dish for my family. I like it so much, in fact, that I serve everyone the fluffy top part and when I'm back in the kitchen I scrape that part off and serve it to myself.

SERVES 8

1 (15-ounce) can green pigeon peas, rinsed and drained
1 cup jasmine rice
¼ cup chopped onion
1 teaspoon grated lemon zest
¼ teaspoon ground ginger
1 garlic clove, minced
¼ teaspoon ground cumin

Combine 3 cups water with the peas, rice, onion, lemon zest, ginger, garlic, and cumin in a medium skillet set over high heat. Bring the mixture to a boil, reduce the heat to low, and simmer for 15 minutes.

INDIAN GREEN PEAS WITH PANEER
An Arranged Marriage

My friend Gori grew up in India. She led quite a jet-setting life as a stewardess for Air India when she was just out of school. Her parents wanted her to settle down and marry, so they placed ads in the matrimonial classifieds. For three years she went out on chaperoned blind dates. Then she met Suresh. It was love at first sight and their families heartily approved. Suresh had grown up in Greenwood, Mississippi, and he brought his new bride home to the Delta. Gori taught me how to make this dish. When we get together to cook I make her tell me their love story just about every time.

SERVES 2

1 cup shelled fresh or frozen green peas

¼ pound paneer (Indian cottage cheese), cubed

1 tablespoon ghee, clarified butter, or vegetable oil

½ teaspoon ground cumin

½ teaspoon ground turmeric

2 bay leaves

1 cinnamon stick

½ cup grated onion

1 teaspoon grated peeled fresh ginger

1 garlic clove, minced

¼ teaspoon salt

2 tomatoes, seeded and chopped

¼ cup plain yogurt

½ teaspoon garam masala (see Note)

¼ cup chopped fresh cilantro

Cook the peas in boiling salted water for 2 minutes or until tender. Drain well and set aside.

Set a large skillet over medium-high heat. Add the paneer and 1 teaspoon of the ghee and cook, turning often, until browned on all sides. Transfer to a bowl of cool water; drain and set aside.

Return the skillet to medium heat and add the remaining ghee, the cumin, turmeric, bay leaves, and cinnamon stick. Cook, stirring, for 1 minute. Add the onion, ginger, garlic, and salt and cook, stirring, for 2 minutes or until the onion begins to brown. Add the tomatoes and cook for 2 minutes or until they begin to break down. Stir in the yogurt, peas, and paneer. Add ½ cup water and the garam masala, reduce the heat to low, and simmer for 5 minutes. Discard the bay leaves and cinnamon stick.

Serve with a sprinkling of the cilantro on top.

NOTE
• Garam masala is an intense spice blend used in Indian cooking. Look for it in specialty shops or at your favorite online spice merchant.

SWEET AND SOUR SALSIFY
Unique

This sweet plum-dressed salsify simply tastes like nothing else. It has a unique delicate flavor that you wouldn't expect from such a woody-looking stick.

SERVES 4

1 pound salsify, peeled (see page 66) and cut into matchsticks

2 tablespoons packed light brown sugar

2 tablespoons plum jelly

3 tablespoons seasoned rice vinegar

2 teaspoons vegetable oil

1 teaspoon toasted sesame oil

½ teaspoon salt

¼ teaspoon freshly ground black pepper

In a small saucepan, cook the salsify in boiling salted water for 10 minutes or until tender. Drain and then return the salsify to the pan. Add the brown sugar, jelly, vinegar, vegetable oil, sesame oil, salt, and pepper. Cook over low heat for 3 minutes, stirring, until the liquid thickens into a glaze.

SQUASH BLOSSOMS
Full Bloom

Honeybees get most of the attention, but squash bees do the most work. These busy bees crawl out of their underground nests and get going a good half an hour before the honey team when the squash flowers are in full bloom. Both the male and female squash bees set to the field work gathering nectar from blossoms, but only the females do double duty collecting pollen.

Bees transfer pollen from the male flowers to the female flowers. The first several flowers of a plant are male and will not produce any fruit. By midday the squash blossoms begin to close and the bees return home. Get to work early like these busy squash bees and pick your squash blossoms early in the day.

Squash blossoms filled with herbed goat cheese and fried with a crisp batter are an annual summer event thanks to the hardworking squash bees.

RECIPE CONTINUES

TEMPURA BATTER

2 cups unbleached all-purpose
  flour
½ cup cornstarch
¼ cup rice flour
1 tablespoon baking powder
1 tablespoon salt
1 teaspoon cayenne pepper
3 cups soda water

FILLING

1 (8-ounce) log mild goat
  cheese, softened
2 tablespoons chopped fresh
  chives
2 tablespoons chopped fresh
  basil
1 teaspoon extra-virgin olive oil
Salt and freshly ground black
  pepper

16 squash blossoms
Vegetable oil, for frying

NOTE
• Several blossoms can be fried at a time; just
  be sure not to overcrowd the oil so they can
  brown easily and the oil temperature does not
  drop too much.

PREPARE THE TEMPURA BATTER. Sift together the all-purpose flour, cornstarch, rice flour, baking powder, salt, and cayenne. Whisk in the soda water, a little at a time, until the right consistency is achieved: The batter should coat the back of a spoon, but some should run off the spoon. Let the batter rest in the refrigerator for at least 1 hour.

MAKE THE SQUASH FILLING. Combine the goat cheese, chives, basil, and olive oil in a medium bowl. Season with salt and pepper and mix well. Scoop up 1 tablespoon of the filling and shape into a ball; repeat with the remaining mixture.

Make sure the squash blossoms are well cleaned: Inspect each flower for insects and any browned petals. Open each flower and insert 1 ball of the goat cheese filling. Gently press the filling into the base of the flower. Close the petals and pinch the top to seal. Refrigerate for 30 minutes.

Heat a deep-fryer or a deep pot with 2 inches of oil to 375°F.

Hold a squash blossom by the stem and dip it into the tempura batter, making sure to coat it completely. Let any excess batter drip off. Place the blossom in the oil and fry until golden brown, 1 to 2 minutes, turning often to brown evenly. Remove to a paper-towel-lined plate. Repeat with the remaining blossoms. Serve immediately.

Entrées & Main Dishes

Easy Chiles Rellenos—De Nada

Delicata Browned Butter Crepes—Delicate

Gardener's Pie—No Shepherd

Stuffed Mirliton—Chayotes and Kazoos

Summertime Spaghetti Squash—Pesto Presto

Fried Pan Trout—Estella's Tavern

Broiled Crisp Flounder—Jubilee Run

Crab and Artichoke Omelet—Soufflé

Grilled Frog Legs—A Cold Beer

Prawns in Dirty Rice—Water Wells

Grilled Split Florida Lobsters—Two-Day Sport Season

Quail with Shallot Gravy—Southern Pan Fried

Butter Breast of Chicken—Plump and Sassy

Roasted Pigeons with Bread Sauce—Grain-Finished

Peanut Chicken—Backyard Poultry

Mexican Co-Cola Drumsticks—Myth and Fingerprints

Pepper Steak—Old Junior Pep

Slow-Cooked Beef Short Ribs—Smoky Apple

Blackberry Lamb Chops—Sweet Tart

Sausage Dinner—Sleep Tight

Sweet Pickle Braised Pork Shoulder—Slow-Cooked and Sliced

Jalapeño Rolled Venison Loin—Creamy Roulade

Kibbeh—Deacon Pattnotte

EASY CHILES RELLENOS
De Nada

When I make true chiles rellenos I seem to get every pot and pan in the kitchen piled up in the sink. On occasion, I want the flavor but not the cleanup. I whip up this version in no time with just one baking dish to wash!

SERVES 6

Nonstick cooking spray

1 cup whole milk

4 large egg whites

⅓ cup unbleached all-purpose flour

3 (4-ounce) cans whole green chiles

6 ounces Jack cheese, grated (⅔ cup)

6 ounces sharp Cheddar cheese, grated (⅔ cup)

1 (8-ounce) can tomato sauce

Heat the oven to 350°F. Grease a deep 1½-quart casserole dish with nonstick cooking spray.

In a small bowl, whisk together the milk, egg whites, and flour. Pour the mixture into the prepared baking dish.

Split open the chiles and rinse under cold running water to remove the seeds; drain on a paper towel.

In a small bowl, combine the cheeses; set aside ½ cup of the cheeses for the topping.

Alternate layering the chiles and cheese in the baking dish, submerging them in the egg mixture. Pour the tomato sauce over the top and sprinkle with the reserved cheese. Bake for 1 hour or until the center is set and the egg batter is puffed all around.

DELICATA BROWNED BUTTER CREPES
Delicate

Toasted pecans and browned butter give these delicate crepes a deep nuttiness. Delicata are small squash and I usually plan on one per person plus one extra when I serve them. This is a nice dish for dinner parties because the components can be made ahead of time and assembled right before dinner.

SERVES 4

CREPE BATTER

¾ cup unbleached all-purpose flour, sifted

¼ teaspoon salt

⅛ teaspoon cayenne pepper

3 large eggs, beaten

1 cup whole milk, at room temperature

2 tablespoons browned butter (see Note)

FILLING

5 Delicata squash (1 pound total)

1½ cups heavy cream

2 tablespoons pecan pieces, toasted, plus more for serving

1 tablespoon Bourbon

⅛ teaspoon freshly grated nutmeg

Salt and freshly ground black pepper

2 teaspoons browned butter (see Note)

MAKE THE CREPE BATTER. In a medium bowl, combine the flour, salt, and cayenne. Make a well in the center of the flour and add the eggs. Incorporate the eggs into the flour with a wire whisk just until moistened. Slowly whisk in the milk, then whisk in the browned butter. Allow the batter to rest for 5 minutes, then strain it to remove any tiny lumps. Let the batter rest again for 20 minutes, or as long as overnight in the refrigerator.

Heat the oven to 325°F.

MAKE THE FILLING. Put the squash on a rimmed baking sheet and bake for 1 hour or until the squash can be easily pierced with a fork. Allow the squash to cool.

In a small saucepan set over medium heat, bring the cream to a simmer, lower the heat, and cook until the cream is reduced by half, about 15 minutes. Add the pecans, Bourbon, and nutmeg and season with salt and pepper. Stir to combine.

• To make browned butter, heat 3 tablespoons
unsalted butter in a small pan over medium-
high heat until the foaming subsides and it has
become slightly browned. Keep an eye on it so
it does not burn. You will have about
2 tablespoons browned butter.

Cut the squash in half, remove the seeds, and scoop the flesh into the cream mixture. Simmer until the squash is easily mashed with a fork. Mix well.

To make the crepes, heat an 8-inch nonstick pan over medium heat. Stir the crepe batter. Ladle 2 tablespoons of the batter into the pan while tilting the pan to evenly distribute the batter all over the surface. Cook the crepe just until moisture beads on the surface. Flip the crepe over and cook for 1 to 2 minutes, until just set. Transfer to a plate. Repeat until all the batter is used, stacking the crepes on top of one another. You will have about 12 crepes.

Spread a layer of squash filling over half of each crepe, then fold the crepe into a half-moon. Heat a skillet over medium heat and add 1 teaspoon of the browned butter. Place 2 folded crepes at a time in the pan and cook for 2 minutes. Flip the crepes and cook for 2 more minutes. Transfer the crepes to a plate. Repeat with the remaining butter and crepes. Garnish with toasted pecans and serve at once.

GARDENER'S PIE
No Shepherd

Vegetarian shepherd's pie is a fulfilling dish for a meatless meal. The kidney beans give it some heft.

SERVES 6

MASHED POTATOES

1½ pounds russet potatoes

¼ cup half-and-half

4 tablespoons (½ stick) unsalted butter

¾ teaspoon salt

¼ teaspoon freshly ground black pepper

1 large egg yolk

MAKE THE MASHED POTATOES. Peel the potatoes and cut into ½-inch dice. Put the potatoes in a medium saucepan and cover with salted cold water. Set the pan over high heat, cover, and bring to a boil. Once it is boiling, uncover the pan, reduce the heat to medium-low, and simmer until the potatoes are tender and easily crushed with a fork, 10 to 15 minutes.

Put the half-and-half and butter in a microwave-safe container and microwave until warm, about 35 seconds.

Drain the potatoes and return them, off the heat, to the warm saucepan. Mash the potatoes. Add the half-and-half and butter mixture, salt, and pepper and continue to mash until smooth. Stir in the egg yolk until well combined.

Heat the oven to 400°F.

RECIPE CONTINUES

FILLING

2 tablespoons canola oil

1 cup chopped onion

½ cup chopped green bell pepper

2 carrots, finely chopped

2 garlic cloves, minced

1 teaspoon salt

½ teaspoon freshly ground black pepper

2 tablespoons unbleached all-purpose flour

2 teaspoons tomato paste

1 cup vegetable broth

2 teaspoons chopped fresh rosemary

1 teaspoon chopped fresh thyme

1 (14-ounce) can red kidney beans, rinsed and drained

½ cup fresh or frozen corn kernels

½ cup fresh or frozen shelled green peas

MAKE THE FILLING. In a large skillet set over medium-high heat, heat the oil until it shimmers. Add the onion, bell pepper, and carrots and cook, stirring, just until they begin to take on color, 3 to 4 minutes. Add the garlic, salt, and pepper. Sprinkle in the flour, stir to combine, and continue cooking for another minute. Add the tomato paste, vegetable broth, rosemary, and thyme, and stir together. Bring the mixture to a boil. Add the kidney beans, reduce the heat to low, cover, and simmer slowly for 10 to 12 minutes or until the sauce has thickened slightly. Stir in the corn and peas.

Spread the vegetable mixture evenly into an 11 x 7-inch glass baking dish. Top with the mashed potatoes, starting around the edges to create a seal to prevent the mixture from bubbling up, and smooth with a rubber spatula. Put the baking dish on a parchment-lined rimmed baking sheet. Bake on the middle rack of the oven for 25 minutes or just until the potatoes begin to brown. Transfer to a wire rack and let cool for at least 10 minutes before serving.

STUFFED MIRLITON
Chayotes and Kazoos

A mirliton is a chayote squash or a vegetable pear. It is also the name for instruments in which a voice resonates over a membrane, as in a kazoo. The Carolina Chocolate Drops are bringing the kazoo back in style with their unique take on traditional jug-band music. I am mounting a campaign to bring the squash back too.

SERVES 6

3 mirlitons
8 tablespoons (1 stick) unsalted butter
1 cup chopped onion
1 cup chopped celery
½ cup chopped red bell pepper
½ cup sliced green onions, white and green parts
½ cup diced ham
4 garlic cloves, minced
1 cup chicken broth
1 cup fresh or frozen peeled salad shrimp
¼ cup chopped fresh parsley
Salt and freshly ground black pepper
1½ cups plain dried bread crumbs

Heat the oven to 375° F.

In a large pot, boil the mirlitons in lightly salted water until the flesh is tender, about 6 minutes. Remove from the pot and cool under running tap water. Halve them and, using a metal spoon, remove the seeds and discard. Gently scoop all of the flesh out of the shells. Set the flesh and shells aside.

In a medium saucepan set over medium-low heat, melt 6 tablespoons of the butter. Add the onion, celery, bell pepper, green onions, ham, and garlic. Cook, stirring, for about 10 minutes or until the vegetables are wilted. Add a little of the chicken broth if the mixture becomes too dry. Add the mirliton flesh and cook for 20 minutes. Add the shrimp and parsley and cook for 5 minutes. Remove from the heat and season with salt and pepper. Sprinkle in 1 cup of the bread crumbs.

Mound the stuffing mixture into the mirliton shells. Put the halves in a baking dish and top with the remaining ½ cup bread crumbs. Dot with the remaining 2 tablespoons butter and pour the remaining broth in the baking dish. Bake for 8 to 10 minutes, until the crumbs are golden brown.

SUMMERTIME SPAGHETTI SQUASH
Pesto Presto

Cooking spaghetti squash in the microwave steams the squash and the strands come out nicely—unlike cooking it in a conventional oven, which can cause the strands to bake to the skin. A simple quick fresh pesto is a snappy sauce for the steamed squash.

SERVES 6

1 (3- to 3½-pound) spaghetti squash

½ cup (packed) fresh basil leaves

2 tablespoons freshly grated Parmesan or Romano cheese

2 tablespoons extra-virgin olive oil

¼ cup pine nuts, toasted

1 garlic clove, minced

Salt and freshly ground black pepper

Prick the squash in 3 or 4 places with a fork, put it on a plate, and loosely cover it with plastic wrap. Microwave at full power for 9 minutes. Let the squash stand, still covered, for another 5 minutes.

Meanwhile, make the pesto. Put the basil, cheese, oil, pine nuts, garlic, and salt and pepper to taste in a food processor and pulse until well combined.

Halve the squash and scrape out the seeds. Using a fork, scoop the pulp into a large bowl. Add pesto to taste and toss to combine.

NOTE
• Dried Zante currants that have been soaked in red wine are a nice addition to this dish.

SANDWICH

BUFFALO
PLATES
SANDWICH

PANTROUT
PLATES
SANDWICH

COMBINATION
ALL PLATES

FRIED PAN TROUT
Estella's Tavern

Back when I was in high school we hung out at Estella's Tavern on Moonbeam Street. It had Formica tables, walls covered halfway with variegated shag carpet and then mirrored the rest of the way up, low lighting, and a hell of a jukebox that had the Nat King Cole song "Sweet Lorraine" on it. I remember some very-late-night meals of pan trout (which was most likely whiting) doused with hot sauce, fried, crisp, and served on slices of white bread—completed, of course, by cold beer in a can. Man, oh man, were those delicious!

Pan trout are what we call just about any fish small enough to fit in a little skillet. Giving the fish fillets a coating of white bread crumbs and a good shot of hot sauce whisks me back in time and has me humming "Sweet Lorraine."

SERVES 4

8 whiting fillets
1 tablespoon hot pepper sauce
½ cup unbleached all-purpose
    flour
2 large eggs, beaten
1 cup plain dried bread crumbs
Salt and freshly ground black
    pepper
½ cup lard or bacon grease

Sprinkle the fish with the hot sauce.

Set up three shallow dishes—one with the flour, one with the beaten eggs, and one with the bread crumbs. Season the bread crumbs with salt and pepper. Dredge each fish fillet in flour, then egg, and finally pat in bread crumbs.

Heat the lard in a heavy-bottomed skillet set over medium heat until it begins to shimmer. Working in batches so the pan is not overcrowded, cook the fish for 3 minutes on each side or until the crust is deep brown. Set them to drain briefly on paper towels and serve piping hot.

BROILED CRISP FLOUNDER
Jubilee Run

Out in Galveston Bay right around Thanksgiving the flounder run. The channels and passes that head from the marshy shallows out towards the deep Gulf of Mexico are teeming with the flat fellows on their way back to the gulf for winter. A hook baited with shrimp and an angler patient enough to give the hook time to set can come home with the two-fish limit.

In Mobile Bay in Alabama the flounder run in the spring is called the Jubilee; the fish are so plentiful they can be scooped up by the netful. A dusting of potato starch and seasoning on these and a belly full of aromatics is a jubilant celebration of the flounders' run.

SERVES 1

1 (2-pound) whole flounder, cleaned
1 green onion
1 lemon slice
1 sprig of fresh dill
¼ cup potato starch
Olive oil
1 teaspoon seafood seasoning (I like Penzeys' Florida Seasoned Pepper)
Extra-virgin olive oil, for serving

Heat the broiler with a broiler pan inside the oven.

Rinse the fish well and pat dry with paper towels. Place the green onion, lemon slice, and dill in the cavity. Dust the fish with the potato starch and drizzle with olive oil. Sprinkle the seafood seasoning generously all over the fish.

Remove the hot broiler pan from the oven and drizzle with oil. Put the fish on the pan and broil for 5 minutes or until the skin is browned and the flesh is opaque and flakes with a fork. Serve immediately with a splash of extra-virgin olive oil.

NOTE
• A Southern flounder's left is its "up side."

CRAB AND ARTICHOKE OMELET
Soufflé

Omelets make a wonderful meal any time of day. This omelet is just right for those summer evenings when the next thing you know the sun has just gone down and it's nine o'clock.

SERVES 2

6 large eggs, separated

⅛ teaspoon salt

⅛ teaspoon freshly ground black pepper

6 ounces Gruyère cheese, grated (⅔ cup)

1 tablespoon unsalted butter

1 teaspoon chopped fresh chives

4 marinated artichoke hearts, drained, quartered, and patted dry

¼ pound lump crabmeat

NOTE
• Warmed plates are nice to serve this omelet.

Put the top oven rack about 4 inches from the heat source and heat the broiler.

In a small bowl, combine the egg yolks, salt, and pepper. Add ⅓ cup of the cheese and stir well to combine.

In a large bowl, beat the egg whites with an electric mixer until almost stiff. With a large spatula, fold the yolk mixture into the whites one third at a time.

Melt the butter in a 10-inch ovenproof skillet set over medium heat. When the butter begins to foam a little, spoon the eggs into the skillet. Give the skillet a good shake and spread the eggs lightly with a spatula to form an even layer. Let the omelet cook undisturbed for 1 minute. Gently loosen the edges of the omelet from the side of the pan. Sprinkle the remaining cheese, the chives, artichokes, and crabmeat over the eggs. Transfer the skillet to the oven and broil for 2 minutes or until the cheese is melted.

Remove the skillet from the oven and gently loosen around the edges again. Hold the skillet over a plate and tilt, while loosening the eggs, to fold the omelet onto the plate. Cut in half with a serrated knife.

GRILLED FROG LEGS
A Cold Beer

Frog legs aren't so much an acquired taste (the taste is great—I've never met anyone who did not like them once they tried them) as they just require some getting used to the idea of eating frogs. Cold beer is the thing to drink with frog legs, but it is also a great marinade to flavor and tenderize the meat.

SERVES 2

12 frog legs (6 saddles or
    pairs)
2 (12-ounce) bottles dark beer
¼ cup chopped onion
2 garlic cloves, minced
½ cup olive oil
¼ cup white vinegar
1 tablespoon Worcestershire
    sauce
1 teaspoon salt
½ teaspoon cayenne pepper

Put the frog legs and beer in a large bowl and refrigerate for 1 hour.

Drain the frog legs and pat them dry. Combine the onion, garlic, oil, vinegar, Worcestershire sauce, salt, and cayenne in a bowl and add the frog legs. Cover and refrigerate for 30 minutes.

Heat the grill to medium.

Remove the frog legs from the marinade; discard the marinade. Put the frog legs on the grill, close the top, and grill for 3 minutes. Turn and cook for 3 more minutes or until the meat is opaque at the bone.

NOTES
• A bunch of frogs is called an army.

• We have a two-hour CD recorded out at Pluto of the frogs singing their love songs on a hot, humid night. It is a remarkable symphony of summer.

PRAWNS IN DIRTY RICE
Water Wells

Freshwater prawns farmed in Mississippi are hatched in the nursery and kept in brackish water for three weeks. After that they are moved to fresh artesian well water in the nursery for thirty more days and then are stocked in ponds when the water temperature reaches the mid-sixties. After about four months they have grown large enough to bring to market.

When the prawns are harvested in the fall from the artesian waters I always make a batch of this dirty rice. It is Southern through and through and well seasoned.

SERVES 6

¼ pound bulk pork sausage

1 pound chicken livers, rinsed, trimmed, and finely chopped

1 medium onion, chopped

1 green bell pepper, chopped

3 celery stalks, chopped

3 garlic cloves, minced

1 pound peeled freshwater prawns

4 cups cooked white rice, hot

¼ cup chopped fresh parsley

Salt and freshly ground black pepper

Hot sauce, for serving

In a large, heavy skillet set over medium-high heat, cook the sausage and chicken livers until browned, breaking up any large chunks as you go, 5 minutes. Add the onion, bell pepper, and celery and cook, stirring, until soft, 5 minutes. Add the garlic and prawns and cook for 3 minutes or until the prawns begin to curl slightly and become opaque. Gently fold in the rice and parsley. Season with salt and pepper.

Serve immediately with hot sauce on the side.

GRILLED SPLIT FLORIDA LOBSTERS
Two-Day Sport Season

The Florida Sport Lobster Season is always the last consecutive Wednesday and Thursday in July. All one needs to join this sporting scene is a bully net—a regular net with the handle bent to form a ninety-degree angle. Just trap the lobster beneath the ring of the net, and when he kicks his tail up into the net, sweep him up and swoop him into the boat!

If you keep some of this butter concoction on hand you can be ready to grill just about any seafood with a slather of citrus butter. (It's handy to pack some in the cooler for grilling out because it does not leak like marinades and sauces might.)

SERVES 4

8 tablespoons (1 stick)
    unsalted butter, softened
¼ cup olive oil
2 large shallots, quartered
4 garlic cloves, halved
⅛ teaspoon cayenne pepper
½ teaspoon grated orange zest
Salt and freshly ground black
    pepper
4 Florida spiny lobster tails,
    split in half lengthwise

NOTES
• Serve these tails with steamed vegetables
and bread to take advantage of all that buttery
lobster-flavored sauce that pools on the plate.

• These also go well with Grilled Green Onions
(page 126).

Heat a grill to high.

Put the butter, oil, shallots, garlic, cayenne, orange zest, and salt and pepper to taste in a food processor and pulse until almost smooth. Spread 1 heaping teaspoon of the seasoned butter over each lobster tail.

In a small saucepan set over low heat, melt the remaining seasoned butter; keep warm.

Put the lobster tails, shell side down, on the grill. Reduce the heat to medium and grill for 8 minutes. Turn and grill until the meat is just opaque in the center, about 2 minutes. Serve with the melted seasoned butter.

QUAIL WITH SHALLOT GRAVY
Southern Pan Fried

A mess of greens is the thing to serve with this golden fried covey and gravy.

SERVES 4

8 (4-ounce) whole quail, dressed and breasts boned

1 tablespoon Worcestershire sauce

1 tablespoon dry sherry

½ teaspoon salt

½ teaspoon freshly ground black pepper

3 cups unbleached all-purpose flour

1 tablespoon poultry seasoning

2 tablespoons vegetable oil, or more if needed

1 cup sliced white mushrooms

3 shallots, chopped

1 tablespoon chopped garlic

1 cup whole milk

¾ cup chicken or vegetable broth

2 tablespoons chopped fresh parsley

1 teaspoon fresh thyme

In a large bowl, toss the quail with the Worcestershire sauce, sherry, salt, and pepper.

In a shallow bowl, combine the flour and poultry seasoning. One at a time, dredge the quail in the flour, shaking to remove any excess. Reserve the extra flour.

Heat the oil in a large skillet. Fry the quail in batches until golden brown and cooked through, turning once, 3 to 4 minutes per side. Remove from the pan and drain on paper towels.

Reserve 1 tablespoon fat in the pan with the browned bits. (If the drippings are too dark, wipe out the pan and add 1 tablespoon vegetable oil instead.) Add the mushrooms, shallots, and garlic and cook over medium-high heat until soft, about 4 minutes. Add 1½ tablespoons of the reserved flour and cook, stirring, for 2 minutes. Pour in the milk and broth and cook, stirring constantly, until thickened, 5 to 6 minutes. Add the parsley and thyme and cook for 1 minute. Remove from the heat. Place the quail on a platter and spoon the gravy on top.

BUTTER BREAST OF CHICKEN
Plump and Sassy

The ubiquitous boneless, skinless chicken breast can be the quickest yet most boring, driest meal. Liven up this dinner staple with a bit of lemon zest, moisten it with butter, and crisp it with crumbs.

SERVES 4

4 tablespoons (½ stick) unsalted butter, softened

½ teaspoon grated lemon zest

¼ teaspoon ground white pepper

½ teaspoon salt

4 (5-ounce) boneless, skinless chicken breasts

½ cup unbleached all-purpose flour

1 large egg, beaten

2 cups panko bread crumbs

In a small bowl, combine the butter, lemon zest, white pepper, and salt. Spoon the butter onto a piece of plastic wrap. Shape the butter into a log, wrap tightly in the plastic wrap, and place in the freezer for 5 minutes or until firm.

Put 1 chicken breast between two pieces of plastic wrap and pound to an even thickness, about ¼ inch. Repeat with the remaining chicken breasts. Place one quarter of the butter in the center of each breast and roll the chicken around the butter. Secure each roll with a couple of toothpicks.

Heat the oven to 375°F.

Set up three shallow dishes: one with the flour, one with the beaten egg, and one with the bread crumbs. Dredge each piece of chicken in flour, next dip in egg, then pat in bread crumbs. Set the chicken in a baking dish and bake for 15 minutes or until well browned and the chicken is no longer pink in the center.

Family Pieces

Her grandmother, like many who married right before World War I, would have been horrified to see Minter carrying the Haviland china soup tureen out of the house to a dinner across town. Reasons for the cringing agitation include the possibility the lid would be broken and a lidded dish with no lid would just linger around the breakfront. But Minter, since her mother's passing, has taken to actually using the "good china" every opportunity that arises.

When she was a child spending the summers and holidays with her Atlanta side of the family, the dishes lived in a special closet blended discreetly into the wall of the dining room and came out weekly for Sunday dinner. Over the years since, the Nabob pattern service for twelve, including serving dishes, has relocated several times, spending years boxed beneath a bed and stored in attics and back rooms. Six years, ago when Minter built her home, she conceived open-door cabinets from here to kingdom come to house the dishes and all her other inherited dinnerware. For Minter, who is anything but a sentimental sap, these plates and chargers of porcelain bound her modern home to people and homes long gone. Her family has left her with these and she aims to see them used, and to be reminded on each occasion of times and events she will never be able to ask about now.

For my cousin LeAnne, who has had three houses burn thus far, the china is what always survives. When all the photographs of birthdays and anniversaries are destroyed, the soot can be washed away, the ashes cleared, and the table set. For her these pieces of bone china are the few tangible remains of her past home life. These dishes are memories vitrified.

The sterling silver kitchen spoon with the worn edge gives my aunt Caroline comfort. This spoon has cooked many of the same recipes for more than a hundred years. Slowly, over the decades, the left side curve of the bowl has straightened with the clockwise stirrings of right-handed cooks going through the same motions as Caroline. Feeling the heat or cold conduction to the tip of her tongue is a visceral connection to her personal history. Each time she raises it to her lips to taste for seasonings, she blows a cooling kiss across the spoon and across time.

Inevitably death, occasionally divorce, and unfortunately fall of fortune find family pieces dispersed, divided, and sold off piece by piece. For Katherine and Jamie, estate sales are their line. For more than a decade they have worked the intersection where family pieces are handed off to their next family and go to new homes. They try to remain as sympathetic and professional as possible in what is almost always a time of emotional upheaval for a family. There are the lingering feelings of guilt when a move to assisted living comes, and Katherine and

Jamie help ease that transfer by taking care of things. Recently more sales are being held for baby-boomers wishing to downsize; many learned from dealing with their parents' possessions that even the most beloved of family pieces can become a burden if there is simply no place to keep them. At times the two are called upon to run interference for the family, sparing them the prying questions and accusations: "How could she part with Ethelen's cut glass punch bowl!" It's no one's business but their clients' why they are selling. Jamie and Katherine are nothing if not discreet. These ladies are well versed in the pecuniary value of silver services and fine china. But perhaps the most important service they provide is being knowledgeable, experienced friends in trying times.

In Sara Anne's elegant antiques shop, glass-front cases hold all manner of sterling silver tableware. Dainty asparagus tongs lie beside ice-cream knives, cold-soup spoons, fish forks, and odd servers. Sara Anne does wish the younger generation had a taste for what she considers the finer things. She is encouraged by small trends like giving an engraved cake server as a baby gift, to be used each birthday and then for the distant wedding cake. Silver water goblets have come around in vogue again and she can hardly keep canapé servers in the shop. As Sara Anne says, "Everybody can use a canapé server." She is right, of course. She is also right when she explains how the newly wed will not remember who gave them a setting of their china pattern but will always remember who gave them the lovely hand-engraved serving piece and think of the giver each time they use it. It will become a family piece.

As for me, the Haviland has been stored up in the closet above the stairs for fifteen years, each stack of china salad plates, dinner plates, and dessert plates zipped inside quilted covers. Fiestaware is what graces my table most days. My mother keeps the silver at her house. She knows all the rules, not letting it come in contact with anything rubber and protecting it from the sullying effects of salt, eggs, and fruits. The one piece of silver I keep out is the gravy boat. For me it's enough for most holiday tables. As much as I wish it were more in my nature to take the time to pull out all the stops and set out the finery, it's just not.

My son will recognize a few items as family pieces—the small chocolate pots from my grandmother, the gravy boat with the copper showing through at the edges, and the stout little pig that stirs the mustard pot. My maiden aunt Lina instructed in her will that we were all to gather at her home after the service and draw straws for her worldly possessions. The short straw got the mustard pot. The stories will be handed down as well. Joe will come to see as family pieces, too, the ceramic work of potter friends from across the state. The McCardy tumblers and the deviled-egg plate Janie Mae Collier made are what he will see when he looks back through photos of holidays when he grows up. The same cake stand turns up in volumes of photo albums all the way back to the sepia-toned. I think these will be the pieces he values most.

ROASTED PIGEONS
WITH BREAD SAUCE
Grain-Finished

Plump country pigeons roost on local grain silos fattening themselves up on the wheat or corn that has spilled. My father is a crack shot and regularly shoots doubles at skeeting events. He occasionally does some practice shooting around the silos, bringing home a batch of fat little birds.

In town look for pigeon in the market, not on statuary. Pigeons at the market are called squab. The biggest difference between the two is those squabs have never flown.

SERVES 4

1 large onion
4 whole cloves
2 bay leaves
8 whole black peppercorns
2 cups half-and-half
Salt and freshly ground black pepper
4 (1-pound) whole pigeons or squab
7 tablespoons unsalted butter, softened
3 cups plain dried bread crumbs
Grate of fresh nutmeg

To start the gravy, cut the onion in half and stick the cloves in it (so you can find them later and don't bite down on one). Put the onion, bay leaves, and peppercorns in a saucepan together with the half-and-half and set the pan over medium heat. Season with salt and bring the mixture to a boil. Remove the pan from the heat, cover, and leave in a warm place for 2 hours or more for the half-and-half to infuse.

Heat the oven to 425°F.

Take each bird and cut the backbone out with shears or a chef's knife. Open the birds wide by spreading them with your hands and cracking the ribs by forcefully pressing down on the birds. Carefully slip your fingers under the skin on the wishbone side of the breasts and smear 1 tablespoon of the butter (per bird) underneath. Liberally salt the birds all over.

• It's best to make your own bread crumbs for this sauce. Homemade crumbs will swell and absorb the infused half and half. Storebought crumbs will make the sauce a touch grainy.

• I like to serve these with sautéed spinach or chard. The spiced bread sauce mixes well with the greens.

In a large ovenproof skillet set over high heat, melt 2 tablespoons of the butter. Add 2 of the birds and sear on both sides until browned, about 4 minutes per side. Transfer to a plate and then brown the remaining 2 birds. Fit all the birds snugly breast side up in the skillet and transfer to the oven.

Roast the birds for 15 minutes or until the juices run clear when the thigh is pierced and the leg moves easily. Remove from the oven and let rest for 5 minutes. Season with pepper.

While the birds are roasting, finish the sauce. Remove the onion, bay leaves, and peppercorns from the half-and-half. Set the pan over low heat, stir in the bread crumbs, and add the remaining 1 tablespoon butter. Cook, stirring occasionally, until the bread crumbs have swelled and thickened the sauce, about 15 minutes. Remove bay leaf.

When ready to serve, spoon some of the bread sauce onto each plate and set a roasted bird on each and spoon juices over each bird. Serve the remaining warm sauce alongside.

PEANUT CHICKEN
Backyard Poultry

Chicken coops have sprung up in some of the poshest neighborhoods. Once you become accustomed to eating well-raised chickens it is hard to tolerate flavorless commercially produced fowl. My friends Paul and Angela Knipple raise chickens in their midtown Memphis yard. They feed the chickens protein-rich peanuts; the result is wonderfully rich eggs and a flavorful chicken. Their rooster is named Karen. He was mismarked at delivery.

Peanuts and chicken are found together in Asian dishes. Here those flavors infuse a whole roasted bird.

SERVES 4

5 tablespoons creamy peanut butter
3 green onions, white and green parts, chopped
3 tablespoons soy sauce
2 tablespoons rice vinegar
½ teaspoon cayenne pepper
1 (3- to 4-pound) chicken
1 (1-inch) piece peeled fresh ginger
2 garlic cloves
A handful of fresh cilantro

NOTE
• Carve the chicken and place on a big serving platter of rice and garnish with some fresh cilantro with the pan juices poured all over.

Heat the oven to 450°F.

In a small bowl, combine the peanut butter, half of the green onions, the soy sauce, vinegar, and cayenne. Gently loosen the skin of the chicken and spread half of the paste between the skin and the meat. Rub the rest of the paste all over the outside of the chicken. Put the remaining green onions, the ginger, garlic, and cilantro into the chicken cavity.

Roast the chicken, breast side down, in a roasting pan for about 20 minutes. Reduce the oven temperature to 325°F. and flip the chicken breast side up. Baste with any juices that have accumulated in the pan. Roast for 30 to 40 minutes, until a meat thermometer inserted into the thickest part of the thigh reads 160° to 165°F. and the juices run clear. Let the bird rest for 10 minutes before carving.

MEXICAN CO-COLA DRUMSTICKS
Myth and Fingerprints

Since Mexican-made Coca-Colas have gained a cult following, varied myths have sprung up around the south-of-the-border beverage—everything from the notion that it actually contains cocaine (I would think it would be more expensive if it did) to the rumor that only two people have the top-secret formula for Mexican Coke. I know I like it—and kosher Coca-Cola, too. I suppose it's simply because of the cane sugar used in the recipe instead of the now-standard corn syrup.

These drumsticks are ridiculously sticky and messy to eat. Corral any children after dinner to wash their hands, and inspect them well before you turn them loose in the house or fingerprints will be found all about.

SERVES 6

1 (8-ounce) bottle cola
¼ cup chopped white onion
¼ cup (packed) dark brown sugar
4 garlic cloves
2 tablespoons ketchup
1 tablespoon finely chopped peeled fresh ginger
1 tablespoon yellow mustard
1 tablespoon Worcestershire sauce
1 teaspoon salt
4 pounds chicken drumsticks, trimmed of excess fat
Peanut oil, for frying
2 cups chicken broth

NOTE
• This is a completely redneck takeoff on the soy sauce drumsticks at the Red Lantern restaurant in Sydney, Australia.

Combine the cola, onion, brown sugar, garlic, ketchup, ginger, mustard, Worcestershire, and salt in a large bowl. Add the chicken and toss to coat. Cover and refrigerate for 1 hour.

Remove the chicken from the marinade; set the marinade aside. Pat the chicken dry. In a deep skillet set over medium-high heat, heat 1 inch of peanut oil. Working in batches, fry the chicken, turning occasionally, until the skin begins to crisp and brown, about 7 minutes. Transfer the chicken to paper towels to drain. Discard the oil.

Put the marinade and chicken broth into the skillet and bring to a boil over high heat. Reduce the heat to low and add the chicken. Simmer for 15 minutes, turning once. Transfer the chicken to a serving platter. Boil the sauce, stirring occasionally, for 5 minutes or until thickened slightly. Pour the sauce over the chicken.

PEPPER STEAK
Old Junior Pep

Junior Pepper lived down the road near my great-aunt Carrye, who was a widow. (Almost all the older ladies out that way are widows, it seems.) Junior Pep, as he is known to all, makes the rounds checking on his lady friends a couple of times a week and calling their relatives if anything seems amiss. He has always been a ladies' man. Junior Pep raised cattle and when I think of pepper steak he always comes to mind.

SERVES 4 TO 6

3 tablespoons olive oil

1 (1- to 2-pound) sirloin steak, cut into 1-inch cubes

1 tablespoon unbleached all-purpose flour

2 celery stalks, thinly sliced

1 large onion, thickly sliced

2 cups beef broth

Pinch of red pepper flakes (or dash of hot sauce)

Dash of Worcestershire sauce

Splash of red wine

1 green bell pepper, chopped

1 red bell pepper, chopped

1 yellow bell pepper, chopped

Heat the oven to 350°F.

In a large pan set over medium heat, heat the oil. Add the steak and cook, turning, until well browned on all sides, about 5 minutes total. Transfer the steak to a 2½-quart baking dish.

Stir the flour into the pan drippings. Cook, stirring constantly, until dark brown, about 2 minutes. Add the celery and onion, reduce the heat to medium, and cook until the vegetables are tender, about 5 minutes.

Stir in the broth, red pepper flakes, Worcestershire sauce, and wine. Bring the mixture to a boil. Pour the hot mixture over the steak in the baking dish. Cover with foil and bake for 1 hour.

Add the bell peppers and continue to bake, uncovered, for 30 minutes or until the steak is fork-tender. Baste the steak with sauce as it cooks, if needed.

SLOW-COOKED BEEF SHORT RIBS
Smoky Apple

When tart apple and sweet carrot cook down slowly with smoked paprika they make a savory jam for these fall-off-the-bone tender ribs.

SERVES 4

2 large tart apples, peeled, cored, and chopped

4 carrots, chopped

1 large onion, cut into wedges

3½ pounds bone-in beef short ribs or oxtails

1 cup applesauce

¼ cup cider vinegar

4 garlic cloves, chopped

1 tablespoon Worcestershire sauce

1 tablespoon smoked paprika

1 teaspoon dry mustard

1½ teaspoons salt

1 tablespoon cornstarch

¼ cup apple cider

Put the apples and carrots in a large slow cooker; top with the onion wedges and then the beef.

Combine the applesauce, vinegar, garlic, Worcestershire sauce, paprika, mustard, and salt. Pour the mixture over the beef. Cover the slow cooker and cook on low for 8 to 10 hours, or high for 4 to 5 hours.

Transfer the meat, apples, and vegetables to a serving platter. Pour the juices into a saucepan, bring to a boil over high heat, reduce the heat, and simmer for 5 minutes.

Combine the cornstarch with the apple cider, stirring until the mixture is smooth. Pour into the simmering juices, bring to a boil, and cook for 1 minute or until the sauce becomes thick and clear. Pour the sauce over the meat and serve.

BLACKBERRY LAMB CHOPS
Sweet Tart

I love berries and lamb. The deep flavor of tender spring lamb takes on the essence of first-of-the-season berries, blending a perfect combination of sweetness with just enough tartness to make you pucker up.

SERVES 2

2 teaspoons vegetable oil

¼ cup sliced green onions, white and green parts

2 tablespoons pure maple syrup

⅛ teaspoon ground cloves

1 cup fresh or thawed frozen blackberries

1 tablespoon red wine vinegar

1 tablespoon blackberry liqueur, such as Chambord

½ teaspoon ground allspice

¼ teaspoon salt

¼ teaspoon coarsely ground black pepper

4 (4- to 5-ounce) lamb rib chops, cut 1 inch thick, or 8 (3-ounce) lamb loin chops, cut 1 inch thick

Heat the broiler with a broiler pan in it.

In a large skillet set over medium-low heat, heat the oil. Add the green onions, syrup, and cloves. Add ½ cup of the blackberries. Cook for about 4 minutes or until the berries have disintegrated and the sauce is just slightly thickened. Stir in the vinegar, liqueur, and the remaining ½ cup berries. Remove from the heat.

In a small bowl, stir together the allspice, salt, and pepper and sprinkle evenly over the chops. Broil in the heated pan, turning once halfway through cooking, for 12 minutes or until barely pink in the center.

Transfer the lamb to the skillet with the sauce and spoon some of the sauce over the lamb. Let the lamb rest in the sauce for 10 minutes before serving.

SAUSAGE DINNER
Sleep Tight

This simple batter puffs up in the oven like a popover and envelops the sweet sausage nestled down in it like a snuggly down comforter. This is a family favorite on cold winter Sunday nights.

SERVES 3

⅓ cup whole milk

⅔ cup unbleached all-purpose flour

1 large egg

6 (3-ounce) sweet Italian sausages

1 yellow onion, thinly sliced

1 tablespoon vegetable oil

Salt and freshly ground black pepper

In a measuring cup with a spout, combine the milk with ¼ cup water.

Sift the flour into a small bowl and make a well in the center. Add the egg and, using a whisk, begin to incorporate it into the flour. Slowly add the milk mixture, whisking until the batter is smooth. Set aside to rest.

Heat the oven to 450°F.

Prick the sausages several times with a sharp knife and put them in an ovenproof skillet with the onion, oil, and ½ cup water. Bake for 18 minutes, turning occasionally, until the onions are browned, the sausages have begun to brown, and the water has reduced to just a thin coating in the bottom of the skillet.

Remove the skillet from the oven and pour the batter around the sausages. Season with salt and pepper. Return to the oven and bake for 30 minutes or until the batter is puffed and deep golden brown.

SWEET PICKLE BRAISED PORK SHOULDER
Slow-Cooked and Sliced

This can be cooked in a slow cooker, in a Dutch oven on top of the stove, or in a roasting pan in a 375°F. oven. Pick the way that suits you. Any way you cook it, you will find that the sweet pickle relish and barbecue sauce flavor the meat through and through.

SERVES 6

1 (4½-pound) boneless pork picnic shoulder
2 teaspoons salt
1 tablespoon olive oil
1 cup sweet pickle relish
½ cup barbecue sauce
2 tablespoons vegetable oil

Heat the oven to 375°F.

Pat the pork dry with paper towels and sprinkle it all over with the salt. Heat the olive oil in a large Dutch oven set over medium-high heat until hot but not smoking. Add the pork and brown it on all sides, about 10 minutes total. Add the relish, barbecue sauce, and 2 cups water and bring to a simmer. Cover the pot, then transfer to the oven. Braise the pork, turning it over once, until the center is tender but not falling apart when pierced with a paring knife, 2½ to 3 hours.

Transfer the pork to a cutting board and tent loosely with foil.

Strain the braising liquid through a sieve into a bowl and discard the solids. Skim off any fat that collects on the surface and cover the bowl to keep the liquid warm.

Cut the meat across the grain into 6 slices (each slice may break into 2 or 3 smaller pieces, depending on the part of the shoulder you have; discard any kitchen string if necessary). Heat the vegetable oil in a 12-inch heavy nonstick skillet set over medium-high heat until hot but not smoking, then sear the pork slices in 2 batches, turning over once, until browned, about 3 minutes per batch.

Transfer the pork to plates and spoon some braising liquid over the top. Pass the remaining braising liquid at the table.

JALAPEÑO ROLLED VENISON LOIN
Creamy Roulade

Creamy cheese spiked with jalapeño peppers in this roulade of cumin- and garlic-flavored venison keeps the lean meat moist. This is one of my husband's favorite ways to share his deer harvest each winter.

SERVES 4

¼ cup olive oil, plus more for the pan

¼ cup red wine vinegar

¼ cup diced onion

4 garlic cloves

1 teaspoon salt

½ teaspoon ground cumin

½ teaspoon chili powder

¼ teaspoon ground white pepper

1 (2-pound) venison backstrap (loin)

1 (8–ounce) package cream cheese, softened

3 jalapeño peppers, seeded and diced

In a large bowl, combine the olive oil, vinegar, onion, garlic, salt, cumin, chili powder, and white pepper.

Slice halfway through the loin down the length of the loin. Lay the sliced loin on a piece of plastic wrap. Cover with another piece of plastic wrap. With a meat mallet or pounder, flatten the loin to an even thickness, about ¼ inch. Remove the plastic wrap and put the venison in the bowl with the seasonings. Cover and refrigerate for at least 1 hour and up to 8 hours.

Remove the venison from the marinade and discard the marinade. Lay the venison out flat and pat the surface dry with paper towels. Spread the cream cheese over the top of the meat. Sprinkle with the jalapeños. Roll up the venison to form a long log and secure with toothpicks if needed.

Heat an oiled grill pan over medium heat until hot. Add the venison and cook for 8 minutes, turning often, or until the center reaches 165°F. Transfer the venison to a cutting board and let stand for 2 minutes before slicing into rounds. Serve at once.

KIBBEH
Deacon Pattnotte

Not a designation by the church but a given name, Deacon Pattnotte ran the small grocery market on Grand Avenue in Yazoo City. He smoked meats and sold them sliced by the pound, but one of the most popular items in the store was his kibbeh. A Lebanese meatball of sorts made with ground beef or lamb and cracked wheat flavored with spices, kibbeh is quite a popular dish in the Delta. When making these in quantity, as Deacon did, the basic rule is for each pound of meat you need 1 teaspoon spice, 1 cup bulgur wheat, and 1 grated onion.

MAKES 24 TO 30
EGG-SIZED MEATBALLS

3 cups #3 cracked wheat
1 tablespoon freshly ground
    black pepper
1 tablespoon ground cinnamon
1½ teaspoons ground allspice
Pinch of ground cumin
Pinch of cayenne pepper
3 white onions, grated
3 pounds lean ground beef
    (top round trimmed and
    ground twice)
Vegetable oil, for frying

Put the cracked wheat in a large bowl and cover it with cool water. Soak the wheat for 1 hour.

Stir together the black pepper, cinnamon, allspice, cumin, and cayenne.

Drain the wheat and squeeze out the remaining water. Add the onions and spice blend and stir well to combine. Using your hands, mix in the meat until everything is well distributed and the mixture starts to form a dough. Form egg-size pieces of the meat mixture.

To fry the kibbeh, heat ½ inch oil in a deep skillet. Working in batches, fry the kibbeh, turning to brown evenly on all sides, for 6 minutes or until cooked through. Serve hot or at room temperature.

NOTES
• If desired, tuck a small chip of cold butter and a couple of toasted pine nuts or slivered almonds in the center of each kibbeh while you form them.

• To bake the kibbeh, brush or spritz with olive oil and bake in a 375°F. oven for 15 minutes or until brown.

• My good friend Donny Whitehead is a kibbeh master, always making enough to share.

Desserts & Sweets

Yazoo Soufflé—No Mistake Plantation Daylilies

Charming Cherry Pie—"Cherry Pink and Apple Blossom White"

Satsuma Tart—Roadside Citrus

Custard Pie—Miss Eudora

Chocolate Chiffon Pie—Party Dress

Cantaloupe Mousse—Sweet Sauternes

Poppy Seed Cakes—American Legion

Blackberry Jam Cake—Sweet Celebration

Pineapple Upside-Down Cake—Long Way Away

Carnival Funnel Cakes—Fun Fair

Carrot Cake—Topiary

Chocolate Honey Cake—Honeyboy Edwards

Plum Cheesecake Bars—Interstate Fruit

Peach Shortcake—Keen

Strawberry Crepes—Rosy Cheeks

Butterscotch Pots de Crème—China Cabinets

Rice Pudding with Lemon Sauce—Dated

Figgy Pudding—Clafouti

Big Blackberry Jelly Roll—Long and Short of It

Baked Alaska—Leave It to Them Old Eskimos

Fudge—It's Good! It's Fudge!

Ricotta Dumplings—Warm Blueberry Compote

Floating Island—Isle Dauphine Club

YAZOO SOUFFLÉ
No Mistake Plantation Daylilies

Miss Ethel Smith was a dedicated member of the Mississippi Daylily Society. Her home was No Mistake Plantation and it was a gathering spot for daylily people. In 1983 Miss Ethel developed the 'Yazoo Soufflé' daylily, a ruffle-edged, double, apricot cream flower.

Organic daylilies are edible and make a beautiful addition to desserts, like this one, in which cream and apricots are fluffed up. Even though this dessert is really a mousse I call it a soufflé in honor of Miss Ethel's lilies.

SERVES 6

1 cup dried apricots
2 tablespoons sugar
2 tablespoons apricot brandy
1 tablespoon unflavored gelatin
1 cup heavy cream, cold
6 daylilies, stamens removed

Put the apricots in a small saucepan with ½ cup water and simmer over medium-low heat for 15 minutes. Add the sugar, raise the heat to medium-high, and cook for 5 minutes, keeping an eye on the apricots so that they don't burn.

While the apricots are simmering, in a small bowl, combine 2 tablespoons cold water with the apricot brandy. Sprinkle the gelatin over the mixture and allow it to soften for 3 minutes. Stir the gelatin and set aside.

When the apricots have finished cooking, put them in a food processor or blender and pulse until pureed. Transfer to a bowl and stir in the gelatin. Place the bowl over ice water. Whisk every minute or so for 5 minutes, or until the mixture is cool.

While the apricot puree is cooling, whip the cream until soft peaks form.

• Pick daylilies in the morning, remove the
stamen, and place them in a large zipper-top
food-storage bag until needed later the same
day; if you pick them late in the day they will
close up.

Fold about one quarter of the whipped cream into
the puree to lighten it. Then fold in the rest of the
whipped cream until fully incorporated.

Place 1 daylily in each of 6 dessert flutes or parfait
dishes, stem end down. Spoon or pipe the mousse
into the daylily-lined flutes. Chill for 3 to 4 hours
before serving.

CHARMING CHERRY PIE
"Cherry Pink and Apple Blossom White"

The week of July 9, 1955, "Rock Around the Clock" bumped "Cherry Pink and Apple Blossom White" off the top of the charts. That was the week rock and roll became king. This combination of Granny Smiths and cherries rocks.

MAKES 1 (8-INCH) PIE

2 batches pie dough (see page 202)

3 cups pitted cherries

1 Granny Smith apple, peeled, cored, and diced

¾ cup (packed) dark brown sugar

¼ cup quick-cooking tapioca

½ teaspoon pure vanilla extract

¼ teaspoon pure almond extract

¼ teaspoon ground cinnamon

Grated zest of 1 lemon

⅛ teaspoon salt

1½ tablespoons unsalted butter, cut into bits

1 tablespoon whole milk

Heat the oven to 400°F. Place a baking sheet in the oven as it heats.

Roll half the dough to a ¼-inch thickness. Line an 8-inch pie pan with the dough and trim the overhang to 1 inch. Roll the remaining dough (and scraps) into a 9-inch-long rectangle that's about ¼ inch thick. Cover and set aside.

In a large bowl, combine the cherries, apple, brown sugar, tapioca, vanilla and almond extracts, cinnamon, lemon zest, and salt. Let stand for 20 minutes. Pour into the crust and dot with the butter.

To make a lattice crust, using a rolling cutter or sharp knife, cut eight 1-inch-wide strips of dough. Place 4 strips across the pie, leaving an inch between the strips. Gently fold back every other strip and place another strip of dough crossing the pie in the other direction. Fold the first strip down. Repeat, alternating the pattern. (Just think of those woven construction-paper place mats you made in elementary school.) Flute the edges, removing any excess dough, and brush the top crust with the milk.

Bake the pie on the baking sheet in the oven for 50 minutes or until golden brown. Serve warm.

SATSUMA TART
Roadside Citrus

Satsuma mandarins are a hardy little citrus grown all along the Gulf Coast areas south of I-10 from Satsuma, Texas, on through Satsuma, Alabama, to Satsuma, Florida. The juice is very sweet and low in acid and the fruit easy to strain, with only a seed or two found in each one. Look for satsumas along roadside stands.

MAKES 1 (9-INCH) TART

CRUST
1 large egg white
¼ cup granulated sugar
1½ cups ground Brazil nuts

FILLING
2 satsumas or tangerines
6 large egg yolks
¾ cup granulated sugar
¼ cup fresh lemon juice
4 tablespoons (½ stick) unsalted butter, cut into bits
1 tablespoon orange liqueur, such as Cointreau

NOTE
• If you can't find satsumas, substitute your favorite tangerine or the modern tangelo.

MAKE THE CRUST. Heat the oven to 375°F.

In a small bowl, whip the egg white until it forms soft peaks. Whisk in the granulated sugar and whip until stiff. Fold in the nuts. Spoon into a greased 9-inch tart pan and smooth with a spatula up the sides and over the bottom of the pan. Bake the crust for 6 minutes or until light brown. Remove the crust from the oven and let cool completely on a wire rack.

MAKE THE FILLING. Grate the zest from the satsumas; reserve 2 tablespoons zest. Juice the satsumas; you need ½ cup juice. Whisk together the egg yolks, granulated sugar, lemon juice, and satsuma juice in a bowl. Strain into a heavy stainless-steel bowl or the top part of a double boiler set over, but not touching, simmering water. Whisk the mixture constantly until thick, about 4 minutes. Stir in the 2 tablespoons zest, the butter, and the liqueur. Cover and chill for at least 3 hours or up to 2 days.

TOPPING

1 cup heavy cream

2 tablespoons confectioners' sugar

1 teaspoon orange liqueur, such as Cointreau

MAKE THE TOPPING. In a bowl, whip the cream until it holds soft peaks. Beat in the confectioners' sugar and orange liqueur.

To assemble the tart, spoon the cooled filling into the cooled crust and top with the whipped cream. Chill for 1 hour before serving.

NOTE

• Garnish with extra grated citrus zest, if desired.

Eudora's Kitchen:
COOK'S BOOKS

When I was quite small my great-aunt Lina gave me a book about a dictionary-loving parrot in a shoe store. I had just learned how to write my name and was somewhat incensed to find someone else's name written right inside (in cursive script no less). Just so everyone would know it was *my* book, I Crayola-ed all the pictures of birds sporting spectator pumps and wing-tipped shoes. And I printed my name real big on the very first page. I'm not sure where Lina had gotten that book for me; she was my great-aunt on my grandfather's side. A single lady, she worked at Weber's Chevrolet as the bookkeeper and was very active in Indianola's B&PWC (Business and Professional Women's Club). She might have picked it up through one of their events.

In our family's home, books have never been things that were put up on the shelf. They were your belongings. You lived with them and they became yours once you read them. We are a family that dog-ears, makes checks in margins, underlines, and loses dust jackets (we draw the line at highlighting, however). That shoe-store bird book was mine once I wrote my name inside. Lina had given it to me and in time I learned that the same Eudora Welty who had written her name right inside had given it to me and all children as well.

By junior high school my family moved briefly to Jackson while my father taught at the medical school, and for a time we lived around the corner from Miss Welty in her Belhaven neighborhood. You'd often see her around at the Jitney Jungle #14 grocery or Parkin's Pharmacy or out in her garden. In Mississippi you got your driver's license at fourteen and a half, so we cruised around our neighborhood like most teenagers on a short leash. We would always glance up at the upstairs window or at the one downstairs, obscured by azaleas, with the side-table lamp where we would see her silhouetted. Not on purpose, just when we wound up on her corner. She was well into her seventies by then. I never knew her. I, like most junior high schoolers, had not really read anything by this "elderly" lady neighbor who was mystically canonized while alive. We just kind of hushedly whispered, "Oh, there's Miss Welty," like bird-watchers spotting an orange and olivaceas prothonotary warbler.

That all changed with my reading of "Why I Live at the P.O." around ninth grade. From then on I would sneak peeks through the grocery shelves or linger in the pharmacy, especially along the back wall, where there was a satellite post office. I would find myself dillydallying at the soda fountain, ordering an extra limeade even though I didn't want one at all. A few times her wide blue eyes cast a glance my way and netted my earnest prolonged gaze. She returned a circumspect look as knowing as mine was curious. Her shopping cart came wheeling around the grocery aisle once and caught me eavesdropping by the big square freezer filled with bagged party ice over near the chips and Coca-Colas. This indiscretion was met with her seemly, amused smile. An understanding grin that seemed sympathetic—much like the one of a gangly, preteen girl who loved to listen—crossed her face, though this one was framed by bobbed white hair.

After high school, friends taking college courses at Millsaps College or Belhaven College and I, on occasion, lived in this long-in-the-cuff neighborhood that had recently been abandoned by the upwardly mobiles who thought suburbs offered security. The McMansion was new to these parts then and lord knows there was room to expand; so away they flew, leaving a sidewalked neighborhood situated between colleges and parks. The young families, steadfast homeowners, and artistic and academic types left in this inner-city enclave looked to Miss Welty's home and garden as an anchor of civilization and an assurance of hope. Her quiet presence was treasured and her privacy was protected on a shade-dappled street.

There, in as simple a kitchen as can be, a young Eudora had come of age. The Welty family moved to Pinehurst Street in 1925

when Eudora, the oldest of the children, was a teen and her brothers Edward and Walter were coming up. The Tudor-style home was built on what was then a gravel road and a cow was kept in the backyard. It was designed by the same architect her father, Christian, had commissioned to build the first skyscraper in Mississippi about a mile away. Six months later her father was dead of leukemia.

Eudora's mother, Chestina, was a prolific gardener, and flowers and edibles grew all around. Out the kitchen window *Camellia japonica* bloomed in winter, *Camellia sasanqua* in the summer, roses with romantic names like Fortune's Double Yellow, Mermaid, Silver Moon, and Gloire de Dijon bloomed in the spring, and pomegranates were ready in the fall.

Back in those days just about any ingredient needed from the grocer appeared on the back step and tabs were settled up at the end of the month. Hollers for greens and peas and plums for sale rang in the mornings with the college's carillons and church bells. The times changed around Eudora in the seventy-six years she lived in this home. Miss Welty acknowledged those changes in her work, yet her kitchen stayed pretty much the same, only updating as far as a plug-in refrigerator and a new gas stove. Central air-conditioning was never even a consideration. She finally approved of a window unit in the downstairs sitting room and one for the bedroom after arthritis replaced her manual Royal typewriter with an electric Smith Corona (which she complained sat there and hummed at you, waiting).

Miss Welty developed photographs from her WPA years in the big enameled kitchen sink, working after sunset. There were no streetlights. Right around this time smoke from burning the manuscript of her short story "The Petrified Man" flew up that stove flue, only to be rewritten from memory a year later when Robert Penn Warren of Louisiana State University's *Southern Review* decided it wasn't so bad after all. It was here her agent Diarmuid (pronounced Dermot) Russell finally paid a visit after thirty-three years of correspondence, representation, and friendship when the great state of Mississippi proclaimed Wednesday, May 2, 1972, to be Eudora Welty Day. She coincidentally was awarded the Pulitzer Prize for Fiction for her novella *The Optimist's Daughter* that same week.

Her home is now home to the Eudora Welty Foundation and all is just as she left it. Neat stacks of books cover every flat surface. The bookcases lining the walls in the front rooms cannot hold one more book and range wildly in subject. There is a sense that she may have just stepped out for a moment.

Just the other day I spent an afternoon in the Welty family's kitchen with Eudora's niece Mary Alice White. Her eyelids seem to close a beat longer than a blink and remind you of someone you can't seem to place. The edges of her smile are familiar and conjure up someone. Just like the way a word can be on the tip of your tongue.

There we sat, a hunkered-down pair, in folding chairs right in the middle of that little kitchen off the back of the house. The house is closed to visitors on Sunday and Monday, so we visited without interruption. Mary Alice reached in one of the two plain manila envelopes she cradled in her lap and pulled into the afternoon sun shining through the window above the kitchen sink a cracked, black leather-bound ledger with "Compositions 1930" debossed upon its cover. It was her grandmother Chestina's personal cookbook filled with orderly pages, rimmed in ocher with age. Penciled in the proper script of a schoolteacher, each recipe was exacting in measurements. French Dressing calls for ⅓ teaspoon of paprika, ⅓ teaspoon of dry mustard, and ¼ teaspoon of salt. Hardly a method is given for any of the recipes. These were written back in the day when people knew how to cook.

From the second envelope, Mary Alice, with an index finger wrapped in one of those new stretchy Band-Aids held aloft like a teacup-pinky, brought out Eudora's small, black, plain, leatherette-bound three-ring notebook, probably no larger than six by eight inches. Blue-lined three-ring punched pages had been removed from the small notebook and fed to the manual typewriter. Seems she only made it about a third of the way through this cookbook project. Mary Alice and I got pretty tickled with this. We and just about all the good home cooks we know had started similar projects and lost interest about halfway through.

A small black bent-iron baker's rack stands close to the stove and holds two small shelves of cookbooks. Mary Alice and I decided to start with *The Joy of Cooking* 1952 edition, the one where fellow Mississippi writer William Alexander Percy's *Lanterns on the Levee,* a 1941 Pulitzer finalist, is noted in the Turtle Soup recipe on page 257. Tucked inside were recipe cards written in Eudora's own hand, requested recipes from friends, and ones clipped from newspapers (mostly local, though a few from papers in New York and Washington that she might have picked up in train stations along her travels). Inside *Joy* we found her additions for Spice Bread Pudding, Butterscotch Pudding, and Corn Pudding. Apparently Miss Welty had a fondness for puddings and custards.

Always one for librarianship and organization of the printed word, Miss Welty had written the title and page number of her favorite recipes in several books on the back flyleaf. This made our undertaking as amateur culinary anthro-pologists much easier. (Thank you, Miss Welty.) It gave us something to go on other than spots and spatters and an occasional piece of onion skin. One book by her good friend Winifred Green Cheney, *The Southern Hospitality Cookbook,* contains a preface by Miss Welty, as does *The Jackson Cookbook* put out by the Jackson Symphony League (of which I participated in the Sub-Deb Ball, an altogether different story). In the comb-bound Symphony League book she had penciled in some proofreader's marks on her introduction, which led into a tribute to Miss Welty by Winifred, who honored her with the recipe remarkably titled Squash Eudora, an astounding combination of summer squash, chicken livers, and curry.

Although Miss Welty never touted herself a fine cook, she was a great one for hospitality and most reports of visits from friends and journalists include an offer of home-cooked lunch or a snack of biscuits and preserves or a bowl from a pot of gumbo or shrimp creole simmering on the back of the stove.

It is in the kitchen that stories are told. The comforting sounds and smells of the kitchens of the South are forever preserved in Miss Welty's storytelling. My afternoon with Mary Alice and the clues left on the small shelves of cookbooks in a house filled with books will stay with me forever. Those cookbooks became Eudora Alice Welty's and their stains of use proclaimed them so. She had lived with them and without doubt they had fueled stories around the table and ones read around the world.

CUSTARD PIE
Miss Eudora

To me egg custard pie is an exemplary Southern dessert. Simple vanilla-flavored custard graced with a dusting of grated nutmeg atop a crisp crust is just what I would have served Miss Welty if I had ever had the chance to thank her for how much her stories have meant to me. I would have also thanked her for a gift that I have begun to appreciate, now that I am—for lack of a better term—grown up: the idea that you don't have to leave the place you love and know, that it is not a prerequisite that to understand home you must exile yourself to gain perspective. No, she led by example and temperament. I hope she would have enjoyed this gratitude pie. I think she might have, with her keenness for custards and all. See photograph on page 204.

MAKES 1 (9-INCH) PIE

CRUST

1 cup unbleached all-purpose
 flour
½ teaspoon salt
⅓ cup shortening or lard,
 chilled
1 large egg white, lightly
 beaten

MAKE THE CRUST. In a medium bowl, combine the flour and salt with a fork to knock out any lumps. With fingertips or a couple of forks, cut the shortening into the flour mixture until the pieces are about the size of small peas. Sprinkle 3 table-spoons cold water over the mixture while tossing quickly with a fork until it begins to come together. Gather the dough and shape it into a smooth ball. Flatten into a disk and wrap in waxed paper. Chill the dough for 1 hour or up to 3 days.

Roll the dough into a 10-inch round. Line a 9-inch pie pan with the dough and pat out any air pockets. Fold the edges overlapping the pan under and crimp with your fingers or a fork. Brush the interior of the crust with the egg white. Refrigerate while preparing the filling.

Heat the oven to 350°F.

CUSTARD FILLING

1 cup whole milk

1 tablespoon unsalted butter

1 cup sugar

2 tablespoons unbleached
all-purpose flour

2 large eggs

¼ teaspoon salt

1 teaspoon pure vanilla extract

Whole nutmeg, for grating

NOTES

• To use this crust for a "blind bake," prick the entire interior of the crust thoroughly with the tines of a fork. Bake in a 450°F. oven for 12 minutes. Cool completely on a rack.

• For the smoothest custard, stir, do not whisk, the warm milk into the egg mixture. If you whisk it, it gets a lot of bubbles on top. The bubbles brown too quickly in the oven and make the surface of the pie look like salamander skin. If you do get a lot of bubbles, let the filled crust sit for 10 minutes or so before baking to give the bubbles time to subside.

• So much of the flavor of this pie resides in the freshly grated nutmeg. This is a case where less is more. Using too much nutmeg or pre-ground nutmeg will make the pie taste medicinal and as if it belongs in a convalescent home.

MAKE THE FILLING. In a small saucepan set over medium-low heat, heat the milk and butter until the butter melts.

Meanwhile, in a medium bowl, whisk together the sugar, flour, eggs, and salt until smooth. Pour the warm milk and butter over the sugar mixture and gently stir to combine. Add the vanilla and stir to incorporate.

Pour the filling into the prepared crust. Grate a little nutmeg over the surface of the custard. Bake on the center rack for 35 to 45 minutes, until the pie has completely puffed across the top. Transfer the pie to a wire rack and let cool completely. Refrigerate for 1 hour or until ready to serve.

CHOCOLATE CHIFFON PIE
Party Dress

My favorite party dress is cocoa-powder brown. It has a crinoline slip underneath and I feel all dolled up when I wear it. I kind of look like a chocolate chiffon pie with a ruffle of whipped cream.

MAKES 1 (9-INCH) PIE

CRUST

1¾ cups gingersnap crumbs

2 tablespoons unsalted butter, melted

1 tablespoon granulated sugar

FILLING

2½ teaspoons unflavored gelatin

1 cup whole milk

¼ cup unsweetened Dutch-processed cocoa powder, sifted

¼ cup plus 2 tablespoons granulated sugar

Pinch of salt

4 large egg yolks

3 large egg whites, at room temperature

1 teaspoon pure vanilla extract

1 cup heavy cream

1 tablespoon confectioners' sugar

Semisweet chocolate, for garnish

Heat the oven to 325°F.

MAKE THE CRUST. In a small bowl, combine the gingersnap crumbs, butter, and granulated sugar. Press the crumb mixture into a 9-inch pie pan and bake for 6 minutes. Remove the pan from the oven and cool on a wire rack.

MAKE THE FILLING. In a small bowl, combine the gelatin with ½ cup cool water and let sit for 5 minutes until the gelatin softens and blooms.

In a medium saucepan set over medium-high heat, bring the milk, cocoa, ¼ cup of the granulated sugar, and the salt just to a simmer, stirring constantly. Remove the pan from the heat and add the gelatin, stirring until the gelatin is completely dissolved.

Put the egg yolks into a medium bowl and beat lightly. Gradually, in a slow stream, add ¼ cup of the chocolate mixture to the egg yolks while whisking continually. Pour the chocolate–egg yolk mixture into the pan with the remaining chocolate mixture. Cook, stirring constantly, over medium

RECIPE CONTINUES

heat until slightly thickened, about 8 minutes. Remove the pan from the heat and let cool for about 20 minutes or until barely warm.

Using an electric mixer, in a large bowl, whip the egg whites to soft peaks. Add the remaining 2 tablespoons granulated sugar and the vanilla, and whip to stiff peaks. Gently fold the cooled chocolate mixture into the meringue in three additions.

Spoon the chocolate mixture into the cool pie crust. Cover and refrigerate for 2 hours.

Whip the cream with the confectioners' sugar. Place dollops of cream over the pie. Grate the semisweet chocolate over the pie.

CANTALOUPE MOUSSE
Sweet Sauternes

Sauternes and melon fluff spooned over ripe cubes of cantaloupe make a fabulously mature dessert for a late-afternoon luncheon. When the fruits are at their aromatic best and you want a dessert that is not overly sweet or directed at the kiddies, this comes together with remarkable sophistication.

SERVES 6

1 very ripe cantaloupe, seeded, peeled, and diced

¼ cup turbinado sugar

2 tablespoons sauternes or white grape juice

1 cup heavy cream

¼ cup sliced blanched almonds

Fresh mint sprigs

NOTE

• If you want some pretty silliness when you serve this, use hollowed-out melon wedges as bowls.

In a small saucepan set over medium heat, cook half of the cantaloupe with the sugar and wine until the melon is very soft, about 7 minutes. Puree in a blender or food processor. Let cool completely.

Whip the cream until it holds firm peaks. Fold the cooled puree into the cream. Spoon the mousse over the remaining diced cantaloupe. Serve at once, garnished with the sliced almonds and mint.

POPPY SEED CAKES
American Legion

Miss Moina Michael was born in 1869 in Good Hope, Georgia. She was educated at Lucy Cobb Institute, Georgia State Teachers College, and Columbia University in New York City, quite an accomplishment for a woman of her times. She went on to work as a professor at the University of Georgia. When World War One broke out she left her teaching position to volunteer in the war effort.

When the war was over Miss Moina returned to the University of Georgia, where she taught continuing education classes for disabled servicemen. She conceived a fundraising idea to help the veterans: selling small silk poppies inspired by John McCrae's memorial poem "In Flanders Fields." ("In Flanders fields the poppies blow / Between the crosses row on row.") Miss Moina from then on wore a red poppy to bring attention to the cause of disabled veterans. By 1921 the American Legion had adopted her red poppy as a symbol of remembrance for fallen soldiers.

To me this delicious cake, decorated with red poppies, is as fitting for a patriotic celebration as anything red, white, and blue. Memorial Day is the perfect occasion to serve these poppy seed petits fours.

MAKES 16 SMALL CAKES

CAKES

Nonstick cooking spray

6 tablespoons (¾ stick) unsalted butter, softened, plus more for the pan

1¼ cups cake flour (not self-rising), plus more for the pan

¾ teaspoon baking powder

¼ teaspoon baking soda

¼ teaspoon salt

1 cup granulated sugar

½ cup almond paste

2 tablespoons poppy seeds

MAKE THE CAKE. Heat the oven to 350°F. Spray a 12 x 17-inch jelly-roll pan with nonstick cooking spray. Line the pan with parchment paper. Butter the parchment and dust it with flour, tapping out any excess.

Sift the 1 ¼ cups of flour, the baking powder, baking soda, and salt onto a piece of parchment paper.

Put ¾ cup of the sugar, the almond paste, and the poppy seeds into the bowl of an electric mixer fitted with the paddle attachment. Mix on medium-low speed until the mixture looks like wet sand.

4 large eggs, separated
½ teaspoon pure vanilla extract
½ cup whole milk
½ cup seedless raspberry jam, warmed to a smooth spreading consistency

As a response to McCrae's poem, Moina Michael penned "We Shall Keep the Faith":

Oh! you who sleep in Flanders Fields,

Sleep sweet—to rise anew!

We caught the torch you threw

And holding high, we keep the Faith

With All who died.

We cherish, too, the poppy red

That grows on fields where valor led;

It seems to signal to the skies

That blood of heroes never dies,

But lends a lustre to the red

Of the flower that blooms above the dead

In Flanders Fields.

And now the Torch and Poppy Red

We wear in honor of our dead.

Fear not that ye have died for naught;

We'll teach the lesson that ye wrought

In Flanders Fields.

Increase the speed to medium-high. Add the butter and mix for 2 minutes or until light and fluffy. Add the egg yolks and vanilla and mix well. Add the flour mixture in 2 batches, alternating with the milk. Transfer to a large bowl and set aside.

In a large bowl, whip the egg whites until foamy. Gradually add the remaining ¼ cup sugar, beating until soft peaks form. Fold one third of the egg whites into the batter with a rubber spatula. Gently fold in the remaining egg whites.

Spread the batter into the prepared pan and smooth the top. Bake for 15 minutes or until a wooden pick inserted into the center of the cake comes out clean. Transfer the pan to a wire rack and let the cake cool completely.

Turn the cake out onto a work surface and carefully remove the parchment paper. Cut the cake in half crosswise and spread one half of the cake with the jam; top with the remaining cake half. Refrigerate the cake for 1 hour.

Trim the sides of the cake and cut the cake into 1½-inch squares. Transfer the cake squares to a wire rack set over a rimmed baking sheet.

RECIPE CONTINUES

LEMON GLAZE

8 cups confectioners' sugar,
    sifted

½ cup light corn syrup

1 teaspoon pure vanilla extract

¼ teaspoon pure almond extract

¼ teaspoon pure lemon extract

ICING POPPIES

1¼ cups solid vegetable
    shortening

4 tablespoons (½ stick) unsalted
    butter, softened

2 cups confectioners' sugar,
    sifted

1 tablespoon whole milk

Red and green paste food
    coloring

NOTES
• To get involved in the American Legion's
  Poppy Campaign visit: www.legion-aux.org/
  MO-Programs/Poppy/index.aspx

MAKE THE GLAZE. In a bowl set over simmering water, combine ½ cup water with the confectioners' sugar, corn syrup, and vanilla, almond, and lemon extracts. Whisk until the glaze is very warm and smooth. Let cool for about 8 minutes before using to coat the cake squares.

Ladle the glaze over each piece of cake, spreading it over the top and sides to coat completely and letting the excess drip onto the baking sheet. If the glaze becomes too thick, add hot water, 1 teaspoon at a time, to loosen it. (The excess icing that drips onto the baking sheet can be scraped off, reheated, strained, and reused.) Let the cakes dry completely.

MAKE THE ICING POPPIES. In a medium bowl, beat together the shortening and butter with an electric mixer. Gradually add the confectioners' sugar, 1 cup at a time, beating well on medium speed after each addition and scraping the sides and bottom of the bowl often. When all the sugar is mixed in, the icing will appear dry. Add the milk and beat at medium speed until light and fluffy. Keep the bowl covered with a damp cloth.

Divide the icing between 2 bowls, one with one third of the icing and the other with two thirds of the icing. With the food coloring, tint the larger amount red and the other green.

Put the icings into parchment paper cones or resealable food-storage bags with a tiny corner cut off. When the cakes are completely dry, pipe poppies onto each cake piece. If desired, place a few poppy seeds in the center of each blossom.

BLACKBERRY JAM CAKE
Sweet Celebration

Spice and fruit and caramel cakes all rolled into one. This cake brings in a lot of money at a bake sale.

MAKES 1 (9-INCH) LAYER CAKE

CAKE

3 cups unbleached all-purpose flour

1 teaspoon baking soda

1 teaspoon ground allspice

1 teaspoon ground cloves

1 teaspoon ground cinnamon

1 teaspoon freshly grated nutmeg

¼ teaspoon salt

1 cup (2 sticks) unsalted butter, softened

1½ cups granulated sugar

1 cup seedless blackberry jam

3 large eggs, beaten

1 cup buttermilk

1 cup chopped pecans

MAKE THE CAKE. Heat the oven to 350°F.

In a medium bowl, sift together the flour, baking soda, allspice, cloves, cinnamon, nutmeg, and salt.

In a separate bowl, beat the butter with an electric mixer. Gradually add the granulated sugar and beat until light and fluffy. Beat in the jam and eggs. Add the flour mixture alternately with the buttermilk, beating until smooth after each addition. Stir in the pecans. Pour the batter into 3 greased and floured 9-inch cake pans and bake for 20 to 25 minutes or until a pick inserted in the center comes out clean. Transfer the pans to a wire rack. Let the cake cool in the pans for 5 minutes, then turn out onto a wire rack to cool completely.

RECIPE CONTINUES

BLACKBERRY CARAMEL ICING

10 tablespoons (1¼ sticks) unsalted butter

¼ cup (packed) light brown sugar

⅓ cup heavy cream

1 tablespoon seedless blackberry jam

1 (8-ounce) package cream cheese, softened

½ teaspoon pure vanilla extract

½ teaspoon salt

1¾ cups confectioners' sugar, sifted

1 pint blackberries, for garnish

MAKE THE ICING. In a saucepan over medium heat, melt 4 tablespoons of the butter and add the brown sugar. Stir until the sugar dissolves. Bring to a boil over medium heat; remove the pan from the heat. Whisk in the cream and blackberry jam until well blended. Transfer to a heat-resistant bowl. Set aside to cool to room temperature, stirring occasionally.

Meanwhile, put the remaining 6 tablespoons butter and the cream cheese in a large bowl. Beat with an electric mixer on medium-high speed until smooth. Beat in the vanilla and salt. With the mixer running, slowly pour in the cooled brown-sugar mixture; beat until smooth. Add the confectioners' sugar gradually, beating well after each addition until completely smooth. Chill slightly for a firmer texture, stirring occasionally.

Place one cake layer on a serving platter. Spread with some of the icing. Repeat with the second and third layers, icing the top of the cake, too. Arrange the blackberries on top.

NOTE
• If all you have in the cupboard is pumpkin-pie spice, use that instead of the individual spices.

PINEAPPLE UPSIDE-DOWN CAKE
Long Way Away

I try to keep my carbon footprint in check and buy local and all, but every now and then I throw caution to the wind and buy a fresh pineapple from a long way away.

Recently I was talking to some fourth-grade kids in the town closest to the farm. Not one out of the fifteen or so kids had ever seen a fresh pineapple other than the one SpongeBob lives in; they just knew they came from a long way away or in a can.

MAKES 1 (8-INCH) CAKE

2 large egg yolks

¾ cup granulated sugar

½ teaspoon salt

½ teaspoon pure vanilla extract

¼ teaspoon pure almond extract

⅓ cup boiling water

1¼ cups cake flour (not self-rising), sifted

1¼ teaspoons baking powder

4 tablespoons (½ stick) unsalted butter

½ cup (packed) dark brown sugar

¼ teaspoon ground cinnamon

1 cup chopped fresh pineapple

NOTES

• This cake topping can be made with most fruits and is very good with blueberries or plums.

• For the best cinnamon flavor, grate some fresh from a stick on a Microplane grater or zester.

Heat the oven to 350°F.

In a medium bowl, beat the egg yolks with an electric mixer for 2 minutes or until thick and lemon colored. Gradually add the granulated sugar and salt while beating on low speed, then add the vanilla and almond extracts. Increase the speed to medium and beat for 1 minute. Slowly add the boiling water while continuing to beat. Turn the mixer off, add the flour and baking powder, and stir until smooth.

In an 8-inch ovenproof skillet set over medium heat, melt the butter with the brown sugar and cinnamon. Cook, stirring, for 1 minute or until the sugar is melted. Remove the pan from the heat and arrange the pineapple in a single layer over the sugar mixture. Pour the cake batter over the pineapple. Transfer the skillet to the oven and bake for 35 minutes or until the cake springs back lightly when touched. Remove the skillet from the oven and let the cake cool for 6 minutes. Invert the cake onto a serving platter and let cool completely.

CARNIVAL FUNNEL CAKES
Fun Fair

We get some real rinky-dink carnivals come through and set up in strip-mall parking lots. We go to every one. We end up blowing more money than we should to win a two-cent stuffed lizard, but I cannot pass up a pick-up duck game. My husband, Donald, always wants to hit the bell with the swing of the sledgehammer and my son, Joe Joe, is keen-eyed when it comes to popping balloons with darts. The smell of the funnel cakes frying up is the smell of fun. You don't have to wait for the sideshow to come to town to enjoy the powdered-sugar goodness that only fried dough can provide.

MAKES 8 INDIVIDUAL
CAKES

2 cups vegetable oil
1 large egg
⅔ cup whole milk
1¼ cups unbleached all-
    purpose flour
2 tablespoons granulated
    sugar
1 teaspoon baking powder
¼ teaspoon salt
Confectioners' sugar,
    for serving

In a deep skillet set over medium-high heat or an electric skillet, heat the oil until it reaches 350°F.

In a medium bowl, beat together the egg and milk. In a separate bowl, combine the flour, granulated sugar, baking powder, and salt. Stir the wet ingredients into the dry ingredients.

Pour the batter into a funnel while holding your finger over the tip, or pour it into a resealable food-storage bag and then snip off one corner. Drizzle the batter into the hot oil, working from the center outwards, making a squiggly spiral. Fry for about 2 minutes per side, then transfer to a wire rack set over a paper-towel-lined baking sheet to drain.

To serve, dust the warm cakes with confectioners' sugar.

CARROT CAKE
Topiary

When you round the curve on Black Hawk Road in hilly Carroll County, you will see it on the left. In four-foot letters the name "Cox" is spelled out in boxwoods. About twenty years ago Mr. Cox started cutting his hedges into all manner of fanciful shapes. He has had a life-size cowboy wearing a Stetson and riding a horse, an alligator, a bird in a cage, and an elephant two times life-size. One of my favorites is a rabbit eating a carrot.

Mr. Cox kind of has the temperament of Mr. McGregor in The Tale of Peter Rabbit. *He has even snipped a self-portrait out of his hedgerow. It looks just like him, with a long beard and a farmer's straw hat perched on his head.*

I love to go out and visit with him. He is a spirited old gent and he lets you know pretty quickly if he is in the mood for company or not. If I bring him a carrot cake, he seems more amiable.

MAKES 1 (9-INCH) LAYER CAKE

CAKE

¾ cup (1½ sticks) unsalted butter, softened, plus more for the pans

3 cups cake flour (not self-rising), sifted, plus more for the pans

1½ teaspoons baking powder

1¼ teaspoons baking soda

1½ teaspoons ground cinnamon

½ teaspoon ground ginger

½ teaspoon salt

1 cup carrot puree (see Notes)

1½ cups buttermilk

1 teaspoon pure vanilla extract

MAKE THE CAKE. Heat the oven to 350°F. Grease three 9 x 1½-inch round cake pans with butter. Line the bottoms with rounds of parchment paper. Butter and lightly flour the paper and the sides of the pans.

Sift the flour, baking powder, baking soda, cinnamon, ginger, and salt into a large bowl.

In a medium bowl, combine the carrot puree, buttermilk, and vanilla.

In a large bowl, with an electric mixer, beat together the butter and granulated and brown sugars at medium speed until light and fluffy. Add the eggs one at a time, beating well after each addition. With

1½ cups granulated sugar

½ cup (packed) light brown sugar

4 large eggs

1¼ cups coarsely chopped pecans

½ cup golden raisins, plumped (see Notes)

CREAM CHEESE ICING

1 (8-ounce) package cream cheese, softened

8 tablespoons (1 stick) unsalted butter, softened

1 tablespoon grated orange zest

1 tablespoon fresh orange juice

1½ teaspoons pure vanilla extract

¼ teaspoon ground cinnamon

1 pound (4 cups) confectioners' sugar, sifted

NOTES

• To puree carrots, bring sliced carrots and a little water to a boil in a medium saucepan. Reduce the heat, cover, and simmer until the carrots are very tender, 15 to 20 minutes. Drain. Puree in a food processor or mash. Four medium carrots (1½ cups sliced) will yield about 1 cup puree. Alternatively, you can use carrot baby food, but it's more expensive.

• To plump up dried raisins, heat the raisins with ½ cup orange juice until the juice begins to simmer. Remove from the heat and let cool. Drain the raisins before adding to the cake.

the mixer on low speed, add the flour mixture alternately with the carrot mixture, beginning and ending with the flour mixture. Stir in the nuts and raisins.

Pour the batter into the prepared cake pans. Bake for 30 to 35 minutes or until a wooden pick inserted near the center of the cake comes out clean and the surface springs back when gently pressed with a finger. Transfer the pans to a wire rack and let cool for 15 minutes. Run a knife around the sides of the cakes to loosen. Turn the cakes out and let cool completely, paper side down.

MAKE THE ICING. In a medium bowl, with an electric mixer on medium speed, beat together the cream cheese, butter, orange zest and juice, vanilla, and cinnamon. Gradually add the confectioners' sugar, beating until smooth.

Place one cake layer on a serving platter. Spread with some of the icing. Place a second cake layer on the first and spread with icing. Place the last cake layer on top and spread the remaining icing over the top and down the sides of the cake.

CHOCOLATE HONEY CAKE
Honeyboy Edwards

Born in 1915 in Shaw, Mississippi, David "Honeyboy" Edwards won a Grammy Lifetime Achievement Award in 2010. He is perhaps the last of the true Delta Bluesmen. Despite his age he keeps on the road touring the world and flirting with the ladies, crooning his hit "Who May Your Regular Be?"

This dense chocolate cake covered with bittersweet honey ganache could be just the thing to win over a loved one's heart or to cure the blues of a broken heart.

MAKES 1 (9-INCH) CAKE

CAKE

8 tablespoons (1 stick) unsalted butter

6 ounces semisweet chocolate, chopped

½ cup honey

4 large eggs, separated

2 tablespoons unbleached all-purpose flour

1 tablespoon instant coffee granules

½ teaspoon baking soda

¼ teaspoon salt

MAKE THE CAKE. Heat the oven to 325°F. Line the bottom of a 9-inch springform pan with parchment paper.

In a medium saucepan set over low heat, melt the butter, then stir in the chocolate. Remove the pan from the heat and continue stirring until the chocolate is completely melted. Gradually add the honey, stirring to blend. Lightly beat the egg yolks, then whisk them into the chocolate mixture. Stir in the flour, coffee granules, baking soda, and salt.

In a large bowl, beat the egg whites until soft peaks form. Fold one quarter of the egg whites into the chocolate mixture. Fold the lightened chocolate mixture into the remaining whites; do not overmix.

Pour the mixture into the prepared pan. Bake for 45 minutes or until a wooden pick inserted near the middle of the cake comes out clean. Transfer the pan to a wire rack and let cool for 5 minutes. Remove the cake from the pan and let cool on a wire rack set over a baking sheet.

HONEY GANACHE

2 ounces semisweet chocolate,
    chopped

2 ounces bittersweet chocolate,
    chopped

½ cup heavy cream

2 tablespoons honey

½ teaspoon pure vanilla extract

MAKE THE HONEY GANACHE. Put both types of chocolate in a medium heatproof bowl.

In a small saucepan set over medium heat, heat the cream and honey until the mixture just begins to simmer. Immediately pour the hot cream mixture over the chopped chocolate and let it sit undisturbed for 1 minute. Stir until all of the chocolate is melted and completely emulsified. Stir in the vanilla.

Pour the warm ganache over the cake, letting the excess drip over the sides and onto the baking sheet. Let set up for at least 30 minutes before serving.

PLUM CHEESECAKE BARS
Interstate Fruit

There is a plum tree on Interstate Highway 35 in Austin, Texas. My uncle Jon keeps an eye on this poor little tree growing in the median. After its showy blooms fade he watches for the red plums. When they look ripe he pulls over with his hazards blinking and picks every last plum and brings them home to make jelly.

MAKES 16 BARS

1¾ cups vanilla wafer crumbs

¾ cup (packed) dark brown sugar

6 tablespoons (¾ stick) unsalted butter, melted

2 (8-ounce) packages cream cheese, softened

⅔ cup granulated sugar

3 large eggs

½ cup plum jelly

½ cup sliced almonds

Heat the oven to 350°F.

In a small bowl, combine the vanilla wafer crumbs, brown sugar, and butter. Set aside ½ cup of the crumb mixture and put the remaining crumbs into a 9 x 13-inch baking dish. Press firmly onto the bottom of the dish.

With an electric mixer, beat the cream cheese, granulated sugar, and eggs on medium speed for 2 minutes or until well blended. Pour the mixture over the crust. Carefully spoon the jelly over the top of the cream cheese mixture. Stir the almonds into the remaining crumb mixture and sprinkle evenly over the jelly.

Bake for 40 minutes or until the center is set and the top is golden brown. Let cool to room temperature. Refrigerate for several hours or until chilled. Cut into bars and serve.

PEACH SHORTCAKE
Keen

I'm keen on freestone peaches. I'm also keen on this shortcake, which comes together quickly. The simple recipe is a great showcase for just about any summer fruits and the little zip of ginger adds a nice dimension.

MAKES 1 (8-INCH) CAKE

1½ pounds fresh peaches or nectarines, peeled and thinly sliced

7 tablespoons (packed) light brown sugar

1 tablespoon Bourbon

¼ teaspoon ground ginger

2 cups unbleached all-purpose flour

1 tablespoon baking powder

½ teaspoon salt

8 tablespoons (1 stick) unsalted butter, cold

⅔ cup whole milk

1 cup heavy cream

¼ cup chopped pecans, toasted

Heat the oven to 425°F.

In a medium bowl, combine the peaches, 4 tablespoons of the brown sugar, the Bourbon, and the ginger. Set the mixture aside while you make the cake.

In a medium bowl, combine the flour, 2 tablespoons of the brown sugar, baking powder, and salt. Using two forks or your fingertips, cut in the butter until the mixture resembles coarse crumbs. Add the milk, stirring only until moistened. Turn the dough out onto a lightly floured work surface. Gently knead 10 times or until the dough comes together and is smooth.

Pat the dough evenly into a greased 8-inch round cake pan. Bake for 20 to 25 minutes, until golden brown. Remove the shortcake from the pan and let cool on a wire rack.

NOTE
• When buying peaches I generally look for freestones. In these varieties, the flesh does not cling to the pit, whereas cling peaches have flesh that does cling and are thus harder to pit.

When ready to serve, whip the cream with the remaining 1 tablespoon brown sugar until stiff peaks form.

Split the shortcake into two layers; place the bottom layer on a serving platter. Spoon half of the peach mixture over the cake and top with half of the whipped cream. Cover with the second cake layer and top with the remaining peach mixture and whipped cream. Sprinkle with the pecans and serve.

STRAWBERRY CREPES
Rosy Cheeks

Dimming the lights and flambéing a dessert tableside makes an exciting end to a meal. If you are doing this for your grand finale at a dinner party, practice in the confines of the kitchen a couple of times first. If your flambé doesn't ignite you might be left blushing tableside. Overdo it on the rum and you will have rosy cheeks for sure.

SERVES 6

2 pints strawberries, hulled and halved
½ cup confectioners' sugar
4 tablespoons dark rum
4 tablespoons (½ stick) unsalted butter
½ cup granulated sugar
12 crepes (see page 148)

Heat the oven to 375°F.

In a medium bowl, toss the strawberries with the confectioners' sugar and 1 tablespoon of the rum. Line a rimmed baking sheet with parchment paper and spread the berries over the paper. Bake for 10 minutes or until the sugar begins to brown and the berries are soft.

Meanwhile, in a large skillet set over medium heat, melt half of the butter. Add the granulated sugar and 2 tablespoons of the rum and stir until combined. One by one, dip each crepe in the butter, making sure to coat both sides. Fold each crepe in quarters while still in the skillet. Arrange the crepes around the outside of the pan. Continue adding more crepes and the remaining butter as necessary. When all 12 crepes have been coated and folded, drizzle the remaining 1 tablespoon rum over the crepes and ignite (be careful). When the flames have subsided, serve while still warm and top with the warm roasted strawberries.

BUTTERSCOTCH POTS DE CRÈME
China Cabinets

Our china cabinet rattles when you walk through the dining room. With each step the lids to my collection of little pot de crème pots remind me that it has been a while since they were used.

SERVES 6

6 large egg yolks
2 cups heavy cream
1 cup whole milk
¼ cup (packed) dark brown sugar
¾ cup granulated sugar
2 tablespoons Scotch whisky
1 teaspoon pure vanilla extract
1 teaspoon salt
¼ teaspoon ground mace

Heat the oven to 300°F.

In a large heatproof bowl, lightly whisk the egg yolks until smooth. Set aside.

In a medium saucepan over medium-high heat, combine the cream, milk, and brown sugar and cook, stirring constantly, until the sugar dissolves and the mixture begins to simmer. Remove the pan from the heat, cover, and keep warm.

In a medium saucepan, combine the granulated sugar with ¼ cup water and bring to a boil over high heat. Cook without stirring until the mixture becomes dark amber, swirling the pan if hot spots develop. Remove the pan from the heat and carefully add the Scotch whisky and ¼ cup of the warm cream mixture, whisking until combined. Whisk in the remaining cream mixture.

Whisk the caramel mixture into the egg yolks in a slow, steady stream. Stir in the vanilla, salt, and mace. Strain the custard through a fine strainer.

RECIPE CONTINUES

Ladle the custard into 6 pot de crème pots or 4-ounce custard cups. Place the cups in a roasting pan and carefully fill the pan with enough hot water to reach halfway up their sides. Cover the pan with foil. Bake for 45 to 50 minutes, until the custards barely jiggle when shaken. Remove the roasting pan from the oven and remove the foil. Allow the custards to cool in the water to room temperature. Transfer the custards to the refrigerator and chill for at least 1 hour.

RICE PUDDING
WITH LEMON SAUCE
Dated

Rice pudding is an old-fashioned dessert and some might consider it dated. I find it a modern comfort. I adore the way chopped dates flavor the creamy sweetened vanilla-infused rice. A drizzle of lemon sauce over the top updates this old-time favorite.

SERVES 6

RICE PUDDING

2 cups cooked rice (I like to use jasmine)

2 cups whole milk

½ cup chopped dates

2 large eggs, beaten

1 tablespoon unsalted butter

½ teaspoon salt

Grate of fresh nutmeg

1 vanilla bean, split

LEMON SAUCE

½ cup sugar

1 tablespoon cornstarch

¼ teaspoon salt

2 tablespoons unsalted butter

1 teaspoon grated lemon zest

2 tablespoons fresh lemon juice

MAKE THE RICE PUDDING. Heat the oven to 325°F.

In a medium bowl, combine the rice, milk, dates, eggs, butter, salt, and nutmeg. Scrape the seeds from the vanilla bean and stir them into the mixture. Pour into a 1½-quart baking dish. Place the dish in a roasting pan and add enough hot water to come halfway up the sides of the baking dish. Bake for 45 minutes or until bubbly around the edges and the top is golden.

MAKE THE LEMON SAUCE. In a small saucepan set over medium heat, combine 1 cup water, the sugar, cornstarch, and salt. Bring the mixture up to a boil. Remove from the heat, add the butter, lemon zest, and lemon juice, and stir well. Drizzle the lemon sauce over each serving of pudding.

Figs Preserve Us

I thought I was Thumbelina. The earliest summer I remember, I had taken to practically living in the summerhouse in my great-grandmother's side yard. About twelve by fourteen feet in size with a thatched roof and walls made of chicken wire paneled in bamboo, this bungalow had once been used as a brooder. Centered in the one room was a hollow brick column where a fire would be built to heat up the brick floor and keep tiny baby chicks warm over cool nights.

Around 1945, after my great-grandmother tired of raising chickens and had moved on from ducks and peafowl, the structure was turned into what I think British folks call a folly, a little garden playhouse. The mortar between the floor bricks had grown over with soft cushiony moss by the time I was coming up. Little brick walkways lined with monkey grass teeming with hop toads and rustling with garter snakes encircled the grounds back to the porte cochere. All was kept cool by the gigantic mimosa tree, festooned with pink, sweet-smelling pompoms, that Momme alternately prized for shade and cussed for upshoots. Ten yards outside the front door of my playhouse, cypress trees sheltered graves of the long-departed Womack family, who had lived here before my great-great-uncle Buddy sold Pluto to my great-great-grandfather in 1933. A baby lamb, the

headstone for the smallest of the lost children, sleeps eternally near brothers and sisters and mother all blanketed in moss. From sunup to sundown this was my little home and garden.

Joseph Newton was my companion during those summer days, Sparrow to my Thumbelina. Born in 1910 on Marcella Plantation, just the other side of Bee Lake, he had gotten on the wrong mule-drawn wagon the day his family moved during a sleet storm in the winter of 1917 and had become lost in the storm—separated from his family for two days. He told me, when I was a little six-year-old girl, how cold and frightened he had been. It was a feeling I could barely imagine, being as spoiled as I was, and yet the thought chilled me.

Across from little Mary Womack's grave stood a grand Celeste fig tree. Joseph would climb up a three-legged orchard ladder while I sat cross-legged beneath that broad-leaved canopy. I would point to a particular fig that struck my fancy and Joseph would pick it and peel it with his sharp Keen Kutter pocketknife. He would hand it down to me with advice and bits of wisdom. The fruit was so warm from the summer's sun it melted in my mouth like a spoonful fished from a batch of just-finished fig preserves.

While riding down Grand Boulevard the other day with my six-year-old son, Joe,

we pulled up next to a beat-up old sixties-model Chevrolet pick up truck. Piled three times higher than the cab and spilling over the sides and dragging on the street were branches and branches from felled fig trees laden with barely ripe fruit. I rolled down the passenger side window and shouted above the rumbling motor, "What the hell happened to that fig tree?" An elderly man with a work-worn face, shaded by a yellow, axle-grease-stained cap—the driver of the truck—shook his head and said, "It's a sin what they's doing in Baptist Town."

"That tree's full a figs!" I exclaimed "Where you takin' 'em?"

"Oh, Miss, I'm taking them to the dump," he replied with sad eyes.

"From where?" I asked as the light turned green.

"By the old compress, they taking 'em all down, Miss, all down," he said again, shaking his head back and forth as he leaned into the turn.

I carried Joe on to school and swung back through Baptist Town. About two hundred homes make up this black neighborhood boundaried by the Illinois Central Railroad, the Columbus & Greenville Railway, and the Pelucia Bayou. And, just as the man said, they were taking down a bushy grove of Celestes.

Celestes are special fruits—really a "false fruit" or synconium, a kind of inside-out flower. With their violet-bronze skin and pear shape, these figs contain no gritty seeds

because the tree is female and does not require pollination to produce. Joseph told me a healthy fig tree would make a fig for every single leaf it has. I would venture to say that a hundred pounds of figs were set out for trash that day, and thousands of future figs. That same week I was up in Minnesota and saw some figs for sale at $12.99 a pound.

This past January I met with a group of enterprising students from Harvard's Kennedy School who are working to devise a plan to help this beleaguered community, and it occurs to me that maybe something as simple as a neighborhood fig harvest could at least raise some money for the cause. I intend to bring it up at the next meeting because there are more fig trees in that neighborhood than I have ever seen anywhere else. This idea is not new; in 1720 figs were introduced to the Louisiana Territory by French missionaries, and Thomas Jefferson was a big proponent of figs. A landowner in Raleigh, North Carolina, reportedly succeeded for a time back in 1910 with figs that "during the past five years netted the owner greater return than any acre in other fruits."

When I questioned the man who seemed to be in charge of the fig tree massacre, he told me with a venomous voice and blank-eyed stare that he was "tired of trying to keep the blackbirds out." The sycophants by his side snarled and nodded.

FIGGY PUDDING
Clafouti

This sweet fig and aniseed pudding is like a clafoutis. The custard bakes to a flan-like consistency and is heavenly served still slightly warm from the oven.

MAKES 1 (8–INCH)
PUDDING

Unsalted butter, for greasing
    the pie pan

½ cup sugar, plus more for the
    pie pan and for sprinkling

6 fresh figs, peeled and halved

3 large eggs, separated

¼ teaspoon salt

1½ cups half-and-half

½ cup unbleached all-purpose
    flour

1 teaspoon brandy

½ teaspoon aniseed

Confectioners' sugar, for
    dusting

Heat the oven to 400°F. Butter an 8-inch deep-dish pie pan and sprinkle with sugar. Place the figs in the dish cut side up.

Whip the egg whites to stiff peaks. In a large bowl, whisk together the sugar, salt, half-and-half, flour, egg yolks, and brandy. Fold the mixture into the egg whites and pour the batter into the prepared dish. Sprinkle the top with a little sugar and the aniseed.

Bake for 20 minutes, then reduce the oven temperature to 350°F., and bake for 10 minutes or until puffy and golden. Dust with confectioners' sugar and serve at once.

BIG BLACKBERRY JELLY ROLL
Long and Short of It

This cake does not take long to bake, yet it looks as if you have gone to a lot of trouble, an impression I like to give. Purchased blackberry jam makes short work of the filling.

SERVES 8 TO 10

Nonstick cooking spray

¾ cup unbleached all-purpose flour, plus more for the pan

4 large eggs

¾ teaspoon baking powder

¼ teaspoon salt

¾ cup granulated sugar

Confectioners' sugar

1 cup blackberry jam

Heat the oven to 400°F. Grease a 15 x 10 x 1-inch jelly-roll pan with nonstick spray and line it with parchment paper. Grease again and flour the paper.

In a large bowl, beat the eggs, baking powder, and salt with an electric mixer on high speed until foamy. Gradually add the granulated sugar, beating until the mixture is thick and lemon colored. Fold in the flour with a rubber spatula and spread the batter into the prepared pan using an offset spatula. Bake for 10 to 12 minutes or until golden.

Sift confectioners' sugar into a 15 x 10-inch rectangle on a clean dish towel. When the cake is done, immediately loosen the sides of the cake and turn it out onto the sugar. Peel off the paper. Starting at the narrow end, roll up the cake and towel together. Transfer to a wire rack, seam side down, and let cool for about 10 minutes.

Very carefully unroll the cake and remove the towel. Spread the cake with the jam and re-roll. Transfer to a serving plate, seam side down, slice, and serve.

BAKED ALASKA
Leave It to Them Old Eskimos

My childhood companion and caretaker Joseph Newton tried to steer us in the right direction. When we were intent on doing something mischievous he would recommend we leave that to them old Eskimos. I have taken to saying this to my little boy, Joe, when he hatches a harebrained scheme.

This dessert is a mindblower for kids and a sort of science experiment all in one. For extra drama, soak sugar cubes in rum and nestle them down in the meringue right when it comes out of the oven. Turn down the lights and light each sugar cube. Wowza.

SERVES 4

2 large eggs

1 cup sugar

1 cup sifted unbleached all-purpose flour

1 teaspoon baking powder

¼ teaspoon salt

½ cup whole milk, hot

2 tablespoons unsalted butter, melted

1 teaspoon pure vanilla extract

1 pint of your favorite ice cream or sorbet, slightly softened (I like strawberry)

1 tablespoon of your favorite fruit preserves (I like orange marmalade)

3 large egg whites

1½ cups marshmallow cream

Heat the oven to 350°F. Butter an 8-inch square cake pan.

In a medium heatproof bowl, beat the eggs with an electric mixer for 3 minutes or until thick and lemon colored. Gradually add the sugar, beating constantly for 4 to 5 minutes.

In a small bowl, sift together the flour, baking powder, and salt. Fold the dry ingredients into the egg mixture. Stir in the milk, butter, and vanilla.

Pour the batter into the prepared pan. Bake for 25 to 30 minutes or until the cake springs back when touched lightly. Cool the cake in the pan for 5 minutes, then turn the cake out onto a wire rack and let cool completely.

Using a 1-quart mixing bowl as a guide, cut out a round of cake. Cut the remaining cake scraps into pieces. Line the bowl with plastic wrap and press the cake scraps in the bottom and up the sides to cover the bowl completely. Put the ice cream on top

- The interior of this mountain of browned meringue is the polar opposite of the ubiquitous molten lava cake. Exploring different flavor combinations is an adventurer's dream. Try lining the bowl with rich vanilla ice cream and then filling the center with orange sherbert for a snow-capped dreamsicle. Lemon sorbet makes a refreshing surprise inside for lemon meringue pie fans. If you hanker for s'mores, go with dark chocolate ice cream. With the ever-expanding variety of premium ice creams out there, the sky is the limit.

- I tend to favor smooth ice creams so there aren't any lumps to interfere with appreciating the strata of sponge cake, cold ice cream, and fluffy meringue.

of the cake scraps, pressing it into the bowl. Brush the cake round with the preserves and place it on the ice cream, brushed side down. Cover the bowl with plastic wrap and freeze for 30 minutes.

To make the meringue, in a medium bowl, whip the egg whites until soft peaks form, about 3 minutes. Gradually add the marshmallow cream, whipping until stiff peaks form.

Remove the bowl from the freezer, unwrap, and unmold the chilled dome onto a foil-wrapped pizza pan. Discard the plastic wrap. Cover the dome with the meringue and freeze for 2 more hours.

To serve, place an oven rack in the lowest position and heat the oven to 500°F.

Remove the dome from the freezer, place on a baking sheet, and bake for 3 to 4 minutes, until the meringue is lightly browned. Serve immediately.

FUDGE
It's Good! It's Fudge!

A plate of fudge passed around the table at the end of a meal is as good a dessert as any. A simple way to form the fudge is to take the box the sugar came in and line it with a plastic bag or use the paper inside the box. Spoon the fudge into the box and let it set— then it is all boxed up and ready to give as a gift!

MAKES 16 (1-INCH)
SQUARES

8 ounces unsweetened
    chocolate (I like Green &
    Black's), finely chopped

3 tablespoons plus 1 teaspoon
    unsalted butter, softened

2 (1-pound) boxes
    confectioners' sugar

2 large eggs, beaten

6 tablespoons heavy cream

2 teaspoons pure vanilla
    extract or favorite
    flavoring

In a bowl set over, but not touching, simmering water, or in a double boiler, combine the chocolate and butter. Stir until melted and smooth. Remove from the heat and add the sugar, egg, cream, and vanilla. Beat the fudge with an electric mixer on medium-low speed until smooth and well blended, about 5 minutes. Spoon the fudge into the prepared box or a buttered loaf pan. Let sit for 1 hour or so to harden. (Or go right ahead and eat some mixed into ice cream!)

RICOTTA DUMPLINGS
Warm Blueberry Compote

These are like sweet little gnocchi wading in a deep purple pool. Aside from being fun to make, the cheese and lemony-mint dumplings play off the sweet, warmly spiced compote and combine into a lighthearted dessert adored by young and old alike. I always like to hide a serving or two away to save for breakfast in the morning.

SERVES 4

DUMPLINGS

1¾ cups whole-milk ricotta, drained (see Notes)

1 large egg

1 large egg yolk

¼ cup finely chopped fresh mint

1 teaspoon grated lemon zest

Grate of fresh nutmeg

⅓ cup unbleached all-purpose flour, plus more for dusting

Salt

BLUEBERRY COMPOTE

2 pints blueberries

½ cup sugar

1 tablespoon unsalted butter

1 teaspoon grated lemon zest

1 cinnamon stick (or ½ teaspoon ground cinnamon)

⅛ teaspoon ground cloves

Grate of fresh nutmeg

MAKE THE DUMPLINGS. In a medium bowl, using a fork, mix the cheese, egg and yolk, mint, lemon zest, and nutmeg. Add the flour and stir with the fork until a dough is formed.

Using two slightly wet spoons or a piping bag, form dumplings (see Notes) and place on a lightly floured baking sheet. After all the dumplings are formed, lightly dust their tops with flour and cover with plastic wrap. Refrigerate for 2 hours or up to 6 hours.

MAKE THE COMPOTE. Cook the blueberries, sugar, butter, lemon zest, cinnamon, cloves, and nutmeg in a saucepan over medium heat, stirring occasionally, until thick and bubbly. Set aside to cool slightly. Remove the cinnamon stick.

When ready to cook the dumplings, bring a large pot of salted water to a boil. Working in batches, gently place the dumplings in the boiling water and cook until they float to the surface, about 3 minutes. Remove with a slotted spoon and transfer to a clean dish towel to drain.

Serve the dumplings in a pool of warm blueberry compote.

NOTES

- Place the ricotta in a colander lined with cheesecloth or a coffee filter and let the excess watery whey drip into a bowl underneath for at least 2 hours in the refrigerator.

- To form the dumplings with dinner spoons, scoop up some of the ricotta mixture with one spoon, and using a second spoon, scrape it onto the floured sheet. To pipe them, use a pastry bag fitted with a ½-inch plain tip to pipe out 2-inch-long dumplings.

- Use a linen dish towel that won't get strings or lint on the dumplings.

- This compote is also awfully good made with stone fruits.

FLOATING ISLAND
Isle Dauphine Club

The Isle Dauphine Club in my youth and at its prime was the toniest of jacket-and-tie-required dinner spots along the Alabama Gulf Coast. My first out-to-dinner memories are of asking the jacketed waiter to describe again Kona Kona Chicken in a Coconut and to his consternation ordering the Spanish Mackerel instead. The place with its swooping lines and gracious curves overlooking the moonlit waters will always be the epitome of dress-up dinner to me. This old-school classic of light poached meringues floating in a caramel gulf is a tribute to the Gulf Coast supper clubs of yesteryear.

SERVES 8

MERINGUES
8 large egg whites
1 cup granulated sugar
1 tablespoon orange liqueur,
    such as Grand Marnier
½ teaspoon pure lemon extract
1 quart whole milk
1 vanilla bean, split and
    scraped
¼ teaspoon grated lemon zest
Grate of fresh nutmeg

MAKE THE MERINGUES. With an electric mixer, whip the egg whites to soft peaks. Gradually add the granulated sugar and continue whipping on high until very stiff peaks form. Whip in the orange liqueur and lemon extract.

In a low, wide pan (such as a deep skillet) over medium heat, bring the milk, vanilla bean and seeds, lemon zest, and nutmeg to a simmer. Using two spoons, form 8 egg-shaped balls of meringue, dropping them into the milk as you form them. Poach for 6 minutes, spooning the milk over the meringues, until the meringues spring back when nudged with the back of a spoon. Using a slotted spoon, remove the meringues to an oiled baking sheet. Strain the milk and reserve it for the caramel sauce.

Heat the oven to 300°F.

CARAMEL SAUCE

2 tablespoons (packed) dark brown sugar

2 teaspoons cornstarch

5 large egg yolks

2 teaspoons Amaretto

¼ cup almond slivers, toasted, for garnish

MAKE THE CARAMEL SAUCE. In a small saucepan set over high heat, cook the brown sugar until it is melted. Carefully pour in the reserved milk and whisk until the caramel is dissolved. Reduce the heat to low. In a small bowl, whisk the cornstarch with the egg yolks. Whisk in a little of the hot milk to warm the eggs. Add the egg mixture to the milk in the saucepan. Cook, stirring constantly, until the mixture begins to bubble, about 3 minutes. Add the Amaretto. Pour into a serving pitcher and keep warm.

Bake the meringues for 5 minutes.

To serve, divide the sauce among 8 shallow bowls. Place a meringue in each dish and sprinkle with toasted almonds.

NOTES

• Separate the eggs a day before to increase the volume of the meringues. Bring whites to room temperature before whipping to reach their full potential: Leave the container on the counter for 30 minutes or place the container in a bowl of warm water to temper.

• Don't tap the whisk against the side of the bowl—it knocks out all the air that you just took so much time to whip in. Tap the whisk instead against your hand to dislodge any meringue that clings.

Acknowledgments

Many a dear friend helped in putting together this collection of recipes. Debra Shaw, Elizabeth Tiedtke, Minter Schenck, Loren Walker, Beth Purifoy, Cathy Thompson, Darby, Sela, Lola and Taylor Ricketts, thank you for the time spent in the kitchen and your generosity.

I'd like to thank my pretty aunt Lucy Wynn for keeping all those sets of china and Sara Anne at Russell's Antiques for keeping up with the silver.

I can never thank my extended family enough for the encouragement each time I come up with a harebrained idea. My cousin Cadi Thompson has been a great support in so many endeavors. It is wonderful to see the kind, generous young woman she has become, and I am honored to have her as a friend.

The collaboration with Chris Granger on the photographic aspects of this book has been a complete joy. Everyone says it and it is true: He is a great guy.

Rica Allannic, my understanding editor, I am forever grateful for the education you have given me. Ashley Phillips, when you come home to Mississippi I'll make you a pie.

Sharon Bowers, as an agent you have worked wonders on my behalf. Thank you.

My deep appreciation goes to the people of the Mississippi Delta and its environs. I am learning more about myself and this place every day and hope my dishes continue to reflect all that you have taught me.

Index